PROPHETIC
MEMORY
IN
WORDSWORTH'S
ECCLESIASTICAL
SONNETS

ANNE L. RYLESTONE

Southern Illinois University Press
Carbondale and Edwardsville

Copyright © 1991 by the Board of Trustees,
Southern Illinois University
All rights reserved
Printed in the United States of America
Edited and designed by Gregory R. Lindenberg
Production supervised by Natalia Nadraga
94 93 92 91   4 3 2 1

Library of Congress Cataloging-in-Publication Data
Rylestone, Anne L., 1946–
    Prophetic memory in Wordsworth's Ecclesiastical sonnets / Anne L.
Rylestone.
        p.   cm.
    Includes bibliographical references.
    1. Wordsworth, William, 1770–1850. Ecclesiastical sonnets.
2. Wordsworth, William, 1770–1850—Religion.   3. Christian poetry.
English—History and criticism.   4. Sonnets, English—History and
criticism.   5. Church history in literature.   6. Great Britain in
literature.   I. Title.
PR5866.R95   1991
821'.7—dc20   89–26352
    ISBN 0–8093–1643–9   CIP

The paper used in this publication meets the minimum requirements of
American National Standard for Information Sciences—Permanence of
Paper for Printed Library Materials, ANSI Z39.48-1984. ♾

Frontispiece, Lord Ashton of Hyde, *Salisbury Cathedral from the
Meadows*, 1831. Photograph courtesy of Lord Thomas Ashton of Hyde.

For Sean

Contents

Acknowledgments

I am grateful for advice on my manuscript from Richard Haven and Howard Brogan of the Department of English at the University of Massachusetts at Amherst and Jean Higgins of the Department of Religion at Smith College. I would also like to thank the Reverend John K. Stendahl of Immanuel Lutheran Church in Amherst, Massachusetts, for his comments on the manuscript and for his advice on religious and historical texts.

I am also grateful to Murray M. Schwartz, Dean of the Faculty of Humanities and Fine Arts, University of Massachusetts at Amherst, for his support.

Special thanks to computer specialist Catherine Hilton, Ph. D., whose technical and linguistic expertise was exceeded only by her capacity for friendship in trying times.

I am indebted to my son Sean Matthew for his patience and emotional support; to James Quentin Knight, D.V.M., for his encouragement and dedicated assistance in practical matters; and to Katie, who faithfully purred and slept on manuscript pages as I worked late into the night.

Introduction

The *Ecclesiastical Sonnets* consist of 132 sonnets that, while
sketching a history of the Christian Church in Britain, dramatize the individual's struggle (including Wordsworth's own as
Christian and poet) with faith and service in the fallen world.
The individual faces a conflicting desire for both individuation
and assimilation into the communal Christian presence that
spans two thousand years of history and extends into an apocalyptic future. The work, in its originality, workmanship, and
philosophical scope, is both a remarkable achievement in English literature[1] and essential to a full understanding of Wordsworth's work as it evolves over the course of more than half a
century.[2]

The series was originally published in 1822 as the *Ecclesias-*
tical Sketches, with most of the sonnets written in 1821.
Wordsworth changed the title in 1837 to the *Ecclesiastical*
Sonnets in Series, and by 1845 he had added thirty sonnets to
the original 102. Although the work is based on the poet's
extensive research of historical and religious texts, it is not,
and does not present itself as, an objective versified historical
account.[3] Readers err when they ignore the objectives set
forth and achieved in the work and instead overemphasize the
Fenwick note (1843), which states that the series merely traces
the history of the Church in England.[4] The work offers Wordsworth's responses, often passionate, to what he deems to be

significant historical, philosophical, and religious issues that arise from this history. His selection and treatment of material provide not only valuable insight into his worldview, but when the work is read with the patience it deserves, the most significant aspect of the *Ecclesiastical Sonnets,* which has been overlooked by critics, becomes clear.

The work portrays the dynamic interaction between collective human experience and the individual's search for identity within the communal historical context. The sonnets reveal the intriguing intellectual, psychological, and artistic processes by which Wordsworth comes to terms with his own Christian identity—processes that are inextricably linked to an internalization of the Christian past, an often dark, entangled, sometimes horrifying, collective memory of the struggle with faith and service in the fallen world. The poet offers his personal endeavor as a model to the reader, highlighting both the uniqueness and the universality of this process, for the journey of reconciliation with the past must ultimately be undertaken alone. The sonnets thus merge the history of self and other, revealing the creation of selfhood as a rigorous process that evolves within sacred and secular historical contexts.[5]

The reader meets the famous and nameless of history in the drama of their lives. Any sense the reader may have of being isolated from them by time is short-lived, for although the poet describes the work as a series of pictures, the scenes remain neither silent nor static. The dramas are vivified by his use of the present tense; people speak and the poet responds as if their delight and sorrow were his own. The reader, drawn into this participation, soon experiences the past as present. In this Wordsworthian synthesis of time, space, and human endeavor, the living panorama achieves a unity, whose cumulative impress imbues the reader with experience and feeling beyond the limitations of his or her own experiential frame of reference. Abbie Findlay Potts, in her critical edition of the work, writes: "The *Ecclesiastical Sonnets* take for granted a polity, both of State and of Church . . . that justice was not an obligation of one man or of one epoch, but the wise, brave, temperate expression of a society rooted in the past and hopeful for the future."[6]

Wordsworth points out in the prefatory letter to the series (24 Jan. 1822, Rydal Mount) that one of the motivations for his writing the *Ecclesiastical Sonnets* was the so-called Catholic Question that arose in Parliament about 1820, dealing with the restoration of civil rights to Catholics. In supporting the High Church party he anticipated the Oxford Movement by a decade, and in the 1830s, he became their "unofficial poet laureate."[7] Although he agreed in 1833 to have the *Ecclesiastical Sonnets* printed "as a book of devotion in verse to accompany Keble's *Christian Year*"[8] and although he spoke with high approval of the Oxford Movement, he did not consider himself a Tractarian and refused a request from Samuel Wilkinson to write in public support of the movement. Wordsworth wrote to Wilkinson: "I rather think that I should better serve the cause we have in common, were I to abstain from what you recommend. It would seem to enroll me as a partisan, and the support which I might otherwise give to Catholic truth would, I fear, in numerous quarters, be impaired accordingly."[9]

Wordsworth's differences with the Oxford Movement highlight his balanced theological position. Mary Moorman writes: "A 'partisan,' in matters of religious doctrine, Wordsworth never was. His view of some of the great Christian beliefs was far 'broader,' and approximated much more nearly to that of Dr. Arnold and even Crabb Robinson and other liberals, than might have been expected of so strong a defender of the Established Church."[10] In a letter to Robinson, for example, Wordsworth writes: "The Atonement is a doctrine which has its foundation in that consciousness of unworthiness and guilt which arises from an upright self-examination—as all orthodox doctrines are warranted by a humble spirit and all that is best in our moral nature." The forgiveness of sin through the Crucifixion of Christ, a theory that Coleridge called "an outrage on common sense," Wordsworth considered "an awful mystery" he was "not called upon to solve."[11]

Wordsworth considered the Church of England the foundation of the nation.[12] In writing the *Ecclesiastical Sonnets* at this time of great social change and political and religious tensions, he may have intended the series to provide a historical context in which readers could better understand the present and shape it with informed, weighed judgments. He could have also hoped that the series, with its emphasis on the strength and unity of the Christian spirit, would instill in people a less partisan point of view and recall them to the Christian ministry of reconciliation.

For Wordsworth, the history of the nation is inseparable from the spiritual history of its people, and in this view, a sense of that history bears profoundly upon the future of humanity. Annabel Newton quotes an anonymous American critic for the *Methodist Quarterly Review* who seems to have read the *Ecclesiastical Sonnets* in 1836 with an insight that has either escaped or not appealed to many subsequent readers:

> [This critic] believes that the labors of Wordsworth have been directed not so much as most readers of the sonnets believed, "to the end of fixing the Establishment more firmly in the affections of the people, but to the far nobler and more congenial purpose of showing that the religion of Jesus Christ contains the only source of genuine happiness, and the only elements of moral progress."[13]

In 1810, the poet writes in his "Reply to Mathetes": "Be it so—let us allow that there is a progress in the Species toward unattainable perfection, or whether this be so or not; that it is a necessity of a good and greatly-gifted nature to believe it" (Owen, 2:11). Wordsworth's belief in the possibility of moral progress infuses the *Ecclesiastical Sonnets* and is articulated directly in this concluding image:

> The living Waters, less and less by guilt
> Stained and polluted, brighten as they roll,
> Till they have reached the eternal City—built
> For the perfected Spirits of the just![14]

Richard E. Brantley writes that the concluding sonnet "sounds for a final time the most inclusive and the most challenging spiritual theme to be heard from both the personal and the public voices of his poetry from the beginning to the end of his career."[15]

The *Ecclesiastical Sonnets* dramatize the reconciliation of the individual with the communal Christian past, the reconciliation of the uniqueness of the individual's faith with its commonality, and the reconciliation of the individual's mortality with his or her oneness with Christ. In a broader perspective, the series attempts to reconcile the ways of men to man so as to unveil in the light of prophetic vision the profound responsibility of the present in the moral progress of humanity.

In this work, the Church joins nature in facilitating the individual's quest for reconciliation. Nature and the Church, which is an institutional expression of elements in the landscape and of links to the past in Wordsworth's other works, serve as intermediaries in the dynamic between the phenomenal and spiritual realities of life in this world.[16] Commenting on *The River Duddon* sonnets, Geoffrey Hartman writes: "The mystery in nature is that of our relation to it, which is darkly sympathetic. . . . The burden of this secret consciousness in Wordsworth should not be underestimated. It is he who stands between us and the death of nature."[17] But in the context of the *Ecclesiastical Sonnets,* it may be more accurate to say that Wordsworth stands between us and the death of God.

Despite this profound role and high praise from a range of critics as Abbie Findlay Potts (1922), O. J. Campbell (1922), Annabel Newton (1928), Edith Batho (1933), A. D. Martin (1936), Mary Moorman (1957), Lee M. Johnson (1973), and Richard E. Brantley (1975), the *Ecclesiastical Sonnets* remain for the most part unread or misunderstood and unjustly maligned. In 1949, for example, Hoxie Neale Fairchild writes:

Detailed analysis of *Ecclesiastical Sonnets* is probably unnecessary and certainly impossible. With a few familiar exceptions, the sonnets are mildly agitated pieces of rhetoric rather than poems. They seldom reveal any personal religious emotion. So far as their ideas are concerned, they give the impression of being the result of collaboration between a humane Protestant who wishes to say all that can justly be said for Catholicism and a humane Catholic who wishes to be equally polite to Protestantism. The plus and minus signs in this travesty of the *via media* cancel out, leaving an intellectual and spiritual zero.[18]

William Sharp (1886) praises Wordsworth along with Shakespeare and Rossetti as "the three greatest sonneteers of our language," and a critic writing for the *American Biblical Repository* (1839) declares the *Ecclesiastical Sonnets* "pre-eminent" among Wordsworth's sonnets, comparable to the sonnets of Milton, but the negative responses seem to be the ones that remain in readers' minds, if they think of the series at all.[19] Perhaps this is a function of selective memory, which provides an excuse not to delve into such a complex and difficult work.

Few would disagree with Moorman when she writes in her admirably balanced discussion of the series that the *Ecclesiastical Sonnets* "are not easy to read."[20] As Wordsworth himself points out, the sonnets "labour under one obvious disadvantage, that they can only present themselves as a whole to the reader who is pretty well acquainted with the history of this country; and, as separate pieces several of them suffer as poetry from the matter of fact, there being unavoidably in all history, except as it is a mere suggestion, something that enslaves the Fancy." He continues, though, with what may serve as advice to a reluctant reader:

> But there are in those Poems several continuous strains, not in the least degree liable to this objection. I will only mention two: the sonnets on the dissolution of the monasteries, and almost the whole of the last part, from the picture of England after the Revolution, scattered over with Protestant churches, till the conclusion. Pray read again from "Open your Gates, ye everlasting Piles" to the end.[21]

Part III of the series, which contains the famous sonnet "Mutability" (III.34), is indeed the most accessible, in part because it is the least historical. Readers new to the work and those returning to refresh their memories may benefit from previewing the heightened energy of the last part. It speaks with the liberated voice of one who has worked through the long and sometimes painful process of assimilating the Christian past and who has also achieved individuation and a clear sense of his own Christian identity. Fortified by a personal and shared faith, he looks to the present and the future of humanity with enthusiasm and hope.

Because of the accessibility of Part III and because approaches to the first part exemplify approaches to the second and third, most of this study (chapters 2 through 6) deals with Part I. Chapter 1 addresses the significance of the *Ecclesiastical Sonnets* to a comprehensive understanding of the body of Wordsworth's works and of his role as poet. Chapter 2 shows how in Part I of the series the epigraph and first two sonnets guide the reader to a viable approach to the entire work's technique and purpose. The subsequent chapters provide a thematic reading of the sonnets, with an emphasis in chapters 3 through 6 on various techniques used to achieve meaning and coherence. Chapter 3 discusses the use of the sonnet set, groups of sonnets linked by narrative, theme, or imagery, and the effective overlapping of these groups. Chapter 4 focuses on the poet's use of language and the powerful role of language in the work's defense of poetry, memory, and revelation through the word/Word. Chapters 5 and 6 highlight the use of imagery and metaphor through which the *Ecclesiastical Sonnets* manifest the synthetic vision set forth in Part II of the series. Chapter 7 examines Part II, which moves the work's synthetic vision of history closer to the present; chapter 8 examines Part III, which thrusts that vision into the present and on into the apocalyptic future.

Prophetic

Memory

in

Wordsworth's

Ecclesiastical

Sonnets

1

The Series in Context

The *Ecclesiastical Sonnets* provide a valuable perspective on the extensive Wordsworthian landscape that evolves over the course of the poet's many works. The Church suddenly imposes itself upon the reader's consciousness, much like a mountain that has long dominated a familiar landscape, but because of some strangeness in the moment, the power of its presence is felt for the first time. The Church represents Christianity in its institutional form, a new focus in the Wordsworth repertoire; but it also represents Christianity manifested in private suffering, endeavor, and spiritual triumph, a theme familiar to the reader of Wordsworth. In this work, the Church looms with a pervading sense of timelessness as an architectural, political, and spiritual force in that otherwise familiar landscape.

The nearly two-thousand-year expanse of British Church history covered by the *Ecclesiastical Sonnets* significantly augments the breadth of human experience dramatized in the vast and varied Wordsworthian landscape. The epic scope of the series, together with its ostensible and inherent purposes, draws the reader to the Gothic church analogy that the poet uses to describe the structural unity of the totality of his works. In the 1814 preface to *The Excursion*, the poet describes *The Recluse*, which was to be the major artistic accomplishment of his life, as analogous to a "gothic church," to which "the

1

preparatory poem" *The Prelude* is to serve as an "ante-chapel."
Wordsworth goes on to say that the "minor Pieces, which have
been long before the Public, when they shall be properly
arranged, will be found by the attentive Reader to have such
connexion with the main Work as may give them claim to be
likened to the little cells, oratories, and sepulchral recesses,
ordinarily included in those edifices."

It is significant that the poet in this 1814 preface views the
cumulative structure and effect of his works as analogous to an
intricate and massive Gothic church and in 1821 begins writing
a verse history of the Christian Church in Britain. While one
Gothic church is not the whole Christian Church, a church
building symbolizes the faith for or by which it is built. As the
concepts of the church as an architectural entity, metaphor,
and symbol begin to coalesce, the reader wonders if that ostensibly unfinished "philosophical poem, containing views of
Man, Nature, and Society; and to be entitled *The Recluse*" is
not ultimately manifested in an exquisite wholeness by the
cumulative impress of Wordsworth's major works—particularly the *Ecclesiastical Sonnets.*[1]

The conclusion of the first book of *The Recluse* demonstrates
some significant parallels between the proposed purpose of
The Recluse and the subject and achievements of the *Ecclesiastical Sonnets.* Crucial in both works are the "sensations and
opinions" of the poet and the dignity of the "individual Mind";
these are linked to the role of faith and the Church in the life
of the individual and the community:

'On Man, on Nature, and on Human life,
Musing in solitude, I oft perceive
Fair trains of imagery before me rise,
Accompanied by feelings of delight
Pure, or with no unpleasing sadness mixed;
And I am conscious of affecting thoughts
And dear remembrances, whose presence soothes
Or elevates the Mind, intent to weigh
The good and evil of our mortal state.
—To these emotions, whencesoe'er they come,
Whether from breath of outward circumstance,
Or from the Soul—an impulse to herself—I
would give utterance in numerous verse.

Of Truth, of Grandeur, Beauty, Love, and Hope,
And melancholy Fear subdued by Faith;
Of blessèd consolations in distress;
Of moral strength, and intellectual Power;
Of joy in widest commonalty spread;
Of the individual Mind that keeps her own
Inviolate retirement, subject there
To Conscience only, and the law supreme
Of that Intelligence which governs all—
I sing:—"fit audience let me find though few!" '2

Aside from providing a challenging and revealing perspective for examining the continuous stream of philosophical, religious, and ethical themes that flow through Wordsworth's work, the *Ecclesiastical Sonnets* play a significant role in completing and unifying the Wordsworth canon. The Church, at its best, serves as a synthesizing force within the characteristically Wordsworthian interdynamic of God, nature, and humanity. The *Ecclesiastical Sonnets* may be seen as the culmination of the drive in Wordsworth's works toward affirmation and philosophical synthesis, demonstrating

How exquisitely the individual Mind
(And the progressive powers perhaps no less
Of the whole species) to the external World
Is fitted;—and how exquisitely, too—
. . . .
The external World is fitted to the Mind;
And the creation (by no lower name
Can it be called) which they with blended might
Accomplish.
(*Recluse*, I.816–19, 821–24)

The integration of nature and the Church is evidenced in the origin of the series and within the work itself. Wordsworth's idea for writing an ecclesiastical history of England arose in part from his walking with Sir George Beaumont on a mild December day in 1820 on Beaumont's estate at Coleorton, with the intention of deciding on a site for a church. Wordsworth writes in the prefatory letter to the series that "it was one of the most beautiful mornings of a mild season,—our feelings were in harmony with the cherishing influence of the scene; to look back upon the past events with wonder and gratitude, and on the future with hope."

The sonnet inspired by this event appears in Part III of the series and embodies Wordsworth's profound skill in integrating the spiritual and phenomenal aspects of human existence. The "native turf" where "rugged colts" and "wild deer bounded" is "by solemn consecration given / To social interests, and to . . . Heaven." The small plot of ground, "infinite [in] its grasp of weal and woe," will encompass the "never-ending ebb and flow" of human endeavor, "trust[ing] / That . . . the Almighty Father looks through all" (III.41). As the church is integrated into the landscape, so too is the range of human experience in the context of nature integrated into the unifying architectural and philosophical structure of the Church.[3]

Within the work, nature and the Church merge in the symbol of the Holy River, whose course represents the history of Christianity. The image naturalizes the Church, while the symbolism humanizes the divine element and deifies the human element. The Church represents a sociological aspect of human culture that links the moral influences of nature to the origin and end of all in the universal spirit. Like nature, the Church is of God but also of humanity—divinely inspired, yet palpable, mortal, and fallen; like the spirit of nature and the soul of humanity, it is immortal and pure.

The introductory sonnet of the series directs the reader to view the work in the context of two of the poet's other works that share the central structural metaphor of tracing the course of a river, *The River Duddon: A Series of Sonnets* (1820) and *Poems Dedicated to National Independence and Liberty* (1815). But to the reader familiar with Wordsworth's work, the poet's charmingly understated reference to only two poems promotes the recollection of an effusion of not only river imagery in his works but water imagery in general. The poet's cross-referencing, context-creating technique reinforces his concern that his readers perceive the unity of his work, as set forth in his great Gothic cathedral analogy and his purposeful arrangement of works in the collected editions.

These ongoing efforts at some point require the discriminating reader to juxtapose the individual work with the larger Wordsworthian context. This approach is more or less useful with all writers, but with Wordsworth it becomes essential because of his conscious and deliberate attempt at interrelation and unity, which he not only asserts but demonstrates by his having one poem refer to another or resonate on a theme or image from another. This contextual approach is, of course, not the only way to read Wordsworth, but it nurtures a comprehensive understanding of the poet's achievement, while encouraging an understanding and an appreciation of the uncanonized works, as well as offering fresh perspectives on familiar ones.

Although space does not permit an extended discussion of water imagery throughout Wordsworth's works,[4] it is worth recognizing the precursor of the Holy River in *The Prelude* and the relationship of that work to the *Duddon* and *Liberty*, and to the *Ecclesiastical Sonnets*.[5] In these four works, linked by central river images, the river serves as a vital source of information that not only stores, but also imposes a coherence on human experience. The river is also a correlative to the presence of the eternality, wisdom, and grace of God in the natural world.

The Prelude opens with the poet wondering where he shall live, asking "what sweet stream / Shall with its murmur lull me to my rest." Attempting to determine his direction, he asks, "shall a twig or any floating thing / Upon the river, point me out my course?" (1805.I.13–14, 29–30). This river imagery attains central importance in *The Prelude* and subsequent works. Wordsworth presents the River Derwent as seminal to his evolution as a poet, and water imagery throughout his work functions as a correlative to the course of development of the poet's mind. *The Prelude* prepares the way for the broader, more objective use of the river image in later works, including the *Duddon, Liberty*, and the *Ecclesiastical Sonnets*.

There is, for instance, a continuity from Book I of *The Prelude* to the introductory poem of the *Ecclesiastical Sonnets*. The music from the personified rivers nurtures him and mediates between the realms of humanity, nature, and God.

Compare the opening lines of the *Ecclesiastical Sonnets* with
the following passage from *The Prelude:*

> —Was it for this
> That one, the fairest of all Rivers, lov'd
> To blend his murmurs with my Nurse's song,
> And from his alder shades and rocky falls,
> And from his fords and shallows, sent a voice
> That flow'd along my dreams? For this, didst Thou
> O Derwent! travelling over the green Plains
> Near my "sweet Birthplace," didst thou, beauteous Stream—
> Make ceaseless music through the night and day
> Which with its steady cadence, tempering
> Our human waywardness, compos'd my thoughts
> To more than infant softness, giving me
> Among the fretful dwellings of mankind,
> A knowledge, a dim earnest, of the calm
> That Nature breathes among the hills and groves.[6]

The *Ecclesiastical Sonnets* begin:

> I, who accompanied with faithful pace
> Cerulean Duddon from its cloud-fed spring,
> And loved with spirit ruled by his to sing
> Of mountain-quiet and boon nature's grace.
> (I.1)

The second passage assumes a recent reading of the *Duddon*
and an easy familiarity with the first passage from *The Prelude*—a familiarity not possible during Wordsworth's lifetime
except to those close to him who had access to the work, but
a familiarity that Wordsworth could anticipate from future
generations; and it would be in character for him to do so.

The water imagery, even in the overtly autobiographical
Prelude, does not remain circumscribed by the poet's personal
development but operates seminally to the profoundly philosophical and objective uses in the subsequent poetry, such as
the Holy River in the *Ecclesiastical Sonnets*. Consider, for
example, the progressive use of water imagery within *The
Prelude*, from the crossing of the Alps passage (Book VI) to the

Snowdon passage and conclusion (Book XIII). Here is the description of the scene after crossing the Alps:

> The immeasurable height
> Of woods decaying, never to be decay'd,
> The stationary blasts of water-falls,
> And everywhere along the hollow rent
> Winds thwarting winds, bewilder'd and forlorn,
> The torrents shooting from the clear blue sky,
> The rocks that mutter'd close upon our ears,
> Black drizzling crags that spake by the way-side
> As if a voice were in them, the sick sight
> And giddy prospect of the raving stream,
> The unfetter'd clouds, and region of the Heavens,
> Tumult and peace, the darkness and the light—
> Were all like workings of one mind, the features
> Of the same face, blossoms upon one tree,
> Characters of the great Apocalypse,
> The types and symbols of Eternity,
> Of first and last, and midst, and without end.
>   (1805.VI.556–72)

The vigor of this passage arises in part from the dynamic elements (blasts of waterfalls, thwarting winds, shooting torrents, drizzling crags, raving stream, unfettered clouds) and from the tension generated by the juxtaposition of the flux with the transcendent stability and eternality of the whole.

The Snowdon passage in *The Prelude* prepares the reader for the images of the Holy River in the *Ecclesiastical Sonnets* by directly merging water imagery with the concept of the divine:

> I looked about, and lo!
> The Moon stood naked in the Heavens, at height
> Immense above my head, and on the shore
> I found myself of a huge sea of mist,
> Which, meek and silent, rested at my feet:
> A hundred hills their dusky backs upheaved
> All over this still Ocean, and beyond,
> Far, far beyond, the vapours shot themselves,
> In headlands, tongues, and promontory shapes,

Into the Sea, the real Sea, that seem'd
To dwindle, and give up its majesty,
Usurp'd upon as far as sight could reach.
Meanwhile, the Moon look'd down upon this shew
In single glory, and we stood, the mist
Touching our very feet; and from the shore
At a distance not the third part of a mile
Was a blue chasm; a fracture in the vapour,
A deep and gloomy breathing-place through which
Mounted the roar of waters, torrents, streams
Innumerable, roaring with one voice.
The universal spectacle throughout
Was shaped for admiration and delight,
Grand in itself alone, but in that breach
Through which the homeless voice of waters rose,
That dark deep thoroughfare had Nature lodg'd
The Soul, the Imagination of the whole.
                                    (1805.XIII.40–65)

But *The Prelude* serves most overtly as a precursor of the imagery in the later works in its concluding image of tracing a river to its source. In defining imagination, the "faculty" that has been "the moving soul / Of our long labour":

                           we have traced the stream
From darkness, and the very place of birth
In its blind cavern, whence is faintly heard
The sound of waters; follow'd it to light
And open day, accompanied its course
Among the ways of Nature, afterwards
Lost sight of it bewilder'd and engulph'd:
Then given it greeting, as it rose once more
With strength, reflecting in its solemn breast
The works of man and face of human life,
And lastly, from its progress have we drawn
The feeling of life endless, the great thought
By which we live, Infinity and God.
                                    (1805.XIII.172–84)

The Prelude concludes, then, with the metaphor of tracing the course of a river, the goal with which the *Duddon, Liberty,* and the *Ecclesiastical Sonnets* begin. As a result, the ostensible objective of tracing a river to its source is a deflection because the stream traced from "the blind cavern" into "open day . . . Among the ways of Nature," lost, then found in "the works" of humanity and in the "face of human life," had already been found in 1805 to culminate and begin in "the great thought / By which we live, Infinity and God." The origin of all rivers is divine, the course of all rivers is through the natural world, and the end of all the searches for sources is the concept of divinity. Perhaps these other searches for origins appear to be posturings because *The Prelude* was posthumously published; however, the goal is not finding the source of these later rivers, but discovering, in the process of the search, the interrelationship of humanity with the natural world and with the creator.

It is in this interpenetration of the spiritual and material worlds that the unity of Wordsworth's work lies. This is not a homogenizing of differences into meaninglessness, but a philosophical and theological approach that generates and thrives on its own energy. This interpenetration relates to the poet's discussion in the 1800 preface to the *Lyrical Ballads* about "the pleasure which the mind derives from the perception of similitude in dissimilitude" and how "upon the accuracy with which similitude in dissimilitude, and dissimilitude in similitude are perceived, depend our taste and our moral feelings."[7] The diversity and bulk of Wordsworth's work reflect the comprehensiveness of this approach.

There is reward in taking the poet seriously when he compares the sum total of his works to a Gothic church. The seemingly disparate, expansive, and complex parts relate overtly, sometimes subtly, to the whole, rewarding the reader who comes to the later poetry remembering that it was written by the same person who wrote *The Prelude*. He is a poet whose central principle throughout is based on the pulsating interdynamic of the phenomenal and spiritual worlds and the human mind, a poet who broods on chaos and the dark so as to create a consciousness of the potential for meaning, hope, love, and joy.

One aspect that to some readers seems to argue against a unified view of Wordsworth's work is the apparent objectification of his approach in later years. By looking at the titles alone, readers can readily accept George Harper's argument that after the *Duddon* sonnets "Wordsworth strove, through his remaining years, to be more objective in his work."[8] This is also verified by a comparison of the topics of works otherwise unified by the river image as a central structural metaphor: *The Prelude*, the *Duddon*, *Liberty*, and the *Ecclesiastical Sonnets*. Topics progress from self-history (autobiography) to history, and there is an evolution toward comprehensiveness in topic even within the "objective" works themselves: political freedom (*Liberty*, 1815), history of a region (*Duddon*, 1820), and Christianity and the Church in England (*Ecclesiastical Sonnets*, 1822).

Some readers relate this comprehensiveness to a loss of poetic power. A discriminating reader might, however, perceive that the vigor of the early work resonates throughout the later poetry. A reader not immediately repelled by "objective" topics may perceive in the later works the poet's enduring personal approach. The centered (but not solipsistic) stance established in *The Prelude*, while personal, is yet universal. It discovers the source of self in divinity, whose correlative is the natural world.

While *The Prelude* is the most overtly personal, its method serves as a model search for self-understanding and integrated experience, achieved through the recognition of the profound interpenetration of nature and the spiritual realm—more specifically, the recognition that a person's relationship with nature can reinforce the connection with the Deity. The process generated in *The Prelude* and augmented in the later works involves an understanding of an individual's development and his or her reconciliation with the past. Fractures in identity can be healed. The past self can merge with the present self, and in this synthetic mode, a way is prepared for the integration of a future self.

The separation of the self into selves, as well as the linear notion of time with its distinctions between past, present, and future, is not a universal concept but is characteristic of Western thought, which emphasizes both categories and linear progress.[9] Wordsworth's vision, while it holds to the notion of moral progress, is, however, synthetic, emphasizing unity and simultaneity. Although he employs linear images such as the river and linear concepts such as history, he uses them to contradict standard cultural notions about the linearity of time and existence. The juxtaposition of the linear image or concept and its nonlinear use generates a dynamic tension in which meaning is suspended. In the *Ecclesiastical Sonnets,* for instance, history becomes not only communal memory but personal experience. In the process of assimilating the past, the distinction between self and other over time dissolves. Yet in this dissolution of individual self into a continuum of all time and space, a new and profound sense of individuation ultimately arises that brings the individual to an acute consciousness of his or her responsibility in the moral progress of humanity.

The theme of the *Duddon* series, as an example of a later work, seems to be a rather objective examination of the history of human life along the river from the time of the original inhabitation to the poet's day. But the work actually perpetuates *The Prelude*'s impetus toward the integrated experience of material and spiritual realms. The poet dedicated the *Duddon* to his brother the Reverend Christopher Wordsworth, Master of Trinity College, Cambridge, a prolific writer of theological works and important in ecclesiastical circles. The *Duddon* series opens with Christmas minstrels' music, while moonlight shimmers on laurel leaves, and offers itself as a source of spiritual refreshment and joy. But the last stanza of the introduction juxtaposes Reverend Wordsworth's possible misjudgment in having chosen a life full of the distractions of the busy world to the wisdom of the poet's living among the rich solitude of nature. In the fourth stanza, the poet says that he "revere[s] the choice / That took thee from thy native hills," but he does not envy it. He views the choice as inviting a potential spiritual death in its inherent separation from nature—as ironic as that may seem addressed to such a prominent theologian.

The later works are more objective in that they examine the interpenetrations of the worlds of nature, humanity, and the spirit. The central importance of the individual remains, how-

ever, evidenced in Wordsworth's focus on individual characters, the accounts of their individual lives, and his response
to these lives serving as a filter and measure of experience.
Although there is a progression toward objectivity in topic,
from self to other, from self-history to history (the accumulated
effect of the stories of individual lives), the poet retains a focus
on the individual and on his perception and integration of that
life into human experience, including his own. The poet of the
Ecclesiastical Sonnets remains true to the definition of a poet
as set forth in the 1802 preface to the *Lyrical Ballads:* "The
Poet binds together by passion and knowledge the vast empire
of human society, as it is spread over the whole earth, and
over all time" (Hayden 1:881).

The objectification, if it can be so named, comes in the
form of emphasis rather than an attempt to remove self and
individual response from the poetry. There is a broad variation
in theme, tone, and dynamics, but the vast symphonic unity
of Wordsworth's work as defined in *The Recluse* perseveres:

> Of Truth, of Grandeur, Beauty, Love, and Hope
> And melancholy Fear subdued by Faith;
> Of blessed consolations in distress;
> Of moral strength, and intellectual Power;
> Of joy in widest commonalty spread;
> Of the individual Mind that keeps her own
> Inviolate retirement, subject there
> To Conscience only, and that law supreme
> Of that Intelligence which governs all—
> I sing:—'fit audience let me find though few!'
> (I.767-76)

A progression that begins in his early work and continues
throughout his works is the transcendence on one level of the
limits of the individual, the community, the nation, the history
of humanity even, to an all-encompassing, shared spiritual
existence, past, present, and future, in the oneness of Christ.
This may seem to be an obvious theme for the *Ecclesiastical
Sonnets*, but the unity in Christ resonates in the early work,
in *The Prelude* most clearly, in the poet's discovering his
chosen status, his divinity, and his duty. The oneness is dem-

onstrated throughout the works in the stories of individual characters evolving and sometimes struggling with their humanity and faith in a fallen yet beautiful world. In the larger context, this is but the history of Christianity, presented as the theme of the *Ecclesiastical Sonnets*.

2

Part I: Reader Orientation—
The Epigraph and Introductory Sonnets

While many readers are misled or put off by the purpose of the series as set forth in the prose attachments and even by the work's title, the epigraph and first two sonnets guide discerning readers to a viable approach to the work. The epigraph addresses the relationship between poetry and piety, preparing the reader for the impress of language in poetry and the Word, and the first two sonnets fulfill multiple functions, not the least of which is portending the unstated but inherent objective of the series: to dramatize the process by which the poet comes to terms with his Christian identity, which is inextricably linked to an internalization of the communal Christian past.

The Epigraph

The epigraph rephrases lines from George Herbert's "The Church-porch"; while Wordsworth's variations intensify the meaning of Herbert's lines, both passages share the message that poetry, because of its beauty, may not only succeed in attracting and teaching a listener when instructional prose may not, but poetry in the psychological and affectual mystery of its workings may evolve the listener's self-surrender and meditational pleasure into piety. The gradual attenuation of self-consciousness on the part of the communicant in this process may imbue the worship with a purer piety than that achieved through a formal church service, an ironic discrepancy also addressed by Herbert in "The Church-porch" (403–26). This efficacy of indirection is reminiscent of Whitman's *Crossing Brooklyn Ferry:* "What the study could not teach—what the preaching could not accomplish is accomplished, is it not?"

Despite the importance of the ecclesiastical architectural metaphor Wordsworth uses to describe the overall structure of his works, it is neither the church building, nor even the institution itself, that plays the most critical religious role. Herbert's lines and Wordsworth's epigraph play ironically upon what is achieved outside the Church toward spiritual ends.

Wordsworth had a strong interest in architecture, especially in buildings fitting in with the surrounding landscape, which may have prompted his use of a synthetic architectural analogy for his works. But in regard to the Church, though he especially admired the powerful effect of church architecture upon the imagination, he focused intently upon the human dynamics that motivate the cultural and individual attraction to the Church in its architectural form and in its institutional and spiritual functions. It is the multifaceted process toward the spiritual life that draws Wordsworth's attention in his poetry. He found all life, even pebbles upon the road, to be a religious experience, with the life of the Church representing but a relevant part of the whole.[1]

Wordsworth's epigraph describes, and perhaps is intended to address, a person with a distracted spirit, who shuns dogma, yet who may undergo an unexpected spiritual renewal through poetry. Wordsworth's five alterations of Herbert's lines from "The Church-porch" intensify the idea of the original, indicating a more determined purpose:

> A verse may finde him, who a sermon flies,
> And turn delight into a sacrifice.
> > —Herbert

> 'A verse may catch a wandering Soul, that flies
> Profounder Tracts, and by a blest surprise
> Convert delight into a Sacrifice.'
> > —Wordsworth

The variation from "finde" to "catch" establishes a more active, assertive process and echoes Jesus' recruiting of the fisherman Simon in Luke 5:10 "henceforth thou shalt catch men." The variation from "him" to "a wandering Soul" (from sonnet III.20, "Baptism") shifts the attention to a person who may not be just temporarily too busy or disinterested to listen, but spiritually lost. "Profounder Tracts" include "sermon[s]," but the term broadens the concept to all written didactic religious doctrine. "By a blest surprise" and "a wandering Soul," in conjunction with the variation from "turn" to "Convert," offer the most significant alterations and intensifications of Herbert's lines. These changes portend the intensity and scope of Wordsworth's intent for the *Ecclesiastical Sonnets:* to embody in the poetry not only a history of the Christian Church in England, but a history of the Christian mystery. Perhaps the understated prose attachments were a deliberate attempt to allow for the "surprise" of the poetry itself.

Herbert's and Wordsworth's lines contain a mysterious power that transcends the limitations of dogma, orthodoxy, and rationality. In versifying the history of the Christian Church in England, the *Ecclesiastical Sonnets* address the ongoing bestowal of grace upon humanity, which for a large part, despite its divine capacities, unfortunately slogs about trying to right things with dogma, orthodoxy, and the rationality of a constricted imagination. After all, the history of a religion is the history of people struggling with circumstances, their own limitations, their untapped capacities, and their faith. But a versified history may actually resonate with the music and mystery of the Word to which humanity, albeit fitfully, aspires.

This enigmatic achievement arises in part from Wordsworth's selection of content and use of poetry. Concerning content, the sonnets do not merely rehash past events; the work is not, as stated in the Fenwick note, "confine[d] . . . to the introduction, progress, and operation of the Church in England, both previous and subsequent to the Reformation." Wordsworth's work does not attempt to replace that of Bede or any of the many other fine ecclesiastical histories. Given the nearly two-thousand-year history of the Church in England, the content of the *Ecclesiastical Sonnets* necessarily offers a rather sketchy account of the Christian chronology. But, in part because of the poet's intense personal engagement with the selected content, the series recreates poignantly the psychological impetus of the Christian mission.

Concerning the use of poetry, the versification imbues the historical account with an imaginative dimension, where past, present, poetry, faith, and the Christian mission coalesce. The music of poetry resonates with the mysterious, ineffable energy that breathes life into human endeavor and lends immediacy to the account. The artistry of the poet's method reasserts the ancient correlation between poetry and piety, wherein the appreciation of the beauty of the poetry becomes sanctified, and the experience becomes an act of devotion.

The epigraph, then, asserts the redemptive power of poetry, its relevance to daily life, and from a broader perspective, the significance of Wordsworth's work to the spiritual evolution of humanity. The *Ecclesiastical Sonnets* are only a part of the interdynamic of all his works, whose "system" may succeed in comforting, perhaps even converting, more souls through poetry than the Church through doctrine. The mission is the same; the method is different. Without having taken formal religious vows, Wordsworth is one of the most religious poets in English literature.

Those readers who come to the *Ecclesiastical Sonnets* expecting a profound tract may find only that. Those who come to the series from Wordsworth's other poetry will find him still the compelling philosophical and psychological strategist who has embodied in this work on the history of the Christian Church in England the history, on a very personal level, of the Christian mystery.

Introductory Sonnet I.1

The introductory sonnet serves five interrelated functions that guide the reader to a viable approach to the series. As discussed in chapter 1, sonnet I.1 places the series in the context of the poet's other work. Sonnet I.1 also introduces the Holy River as the central structural metaphor; it articulates

the ostensible historical purpose of the series, while providing
evidence of a more profound religious one; it establishes a
dynamic interaction among poet, text, and reader; and it prefigures the structure of the series. These functions are discussed in order below.

The Holy River

The Holy River, like the first sonnet, has multiple functions.
As a river image, it serves as a linear but complex representation of time, unifying the series' two-thousand-year span of
history. It grounds the series and Christianity in nature,
achieving an interpenetration of nature and the Church. It
introduces water imagery that appears throughout the series
in various forms, both literal and figurative; this imagery unites
the whole and coordinates groups of sonnets with distinct but
interweaving strands of continuity and suspends the work in
the larger theological context with the biblical implications of
the Flood and baptism. Finally, this image of the Holy River
connects the series with the poet's other works in which water
imagery serves both structurally and symbolically.

Time. The Holy River fulfills its simplest role as a linear
representation of time from the uncertain origins of Christianity in Britain to the poet's present day, with the most recent
historical reference in sonnet III.15 to Bishop White and the
American episcopacy in the late eighteenth century.[2] Much of
the liturgy section in Part III of the series remains current
even today.

The last sonnet of the series, "Conclusion," emphasizes the
work's penetration of the future with two images that are both
linear and cyclical, the rolling of river water and a coiled snake:
"The living Waters . . . brighten as they roll" toward the
Eternal City and the future "sleeps . . . as a snake enrolled, /
Coil within coil, at noon-tide" (III.47). This particularly rich
sonnet is discussed in detail in chapter 8, but suffice it to say
that the river as a representation of time is not simply linearly
progressive—it not only reaches into the future, as far as
incorporating the apocalypse, but the flowing aspect of the
river, its being forever new and yet ancient and potential,

deepens and empowers the present with a revivification of the
past, along with an awareness of the creative potential of the
future. What this means for the poet, as for the engaged
reader, is that a journey along this river involves the internalization of the past in such a way that he comes to terms with
his own Christian identity. This seemingly detached past, this
history of other, becomes, for the Christian united with others
in the body of Christ, his own memory, the history of his own
identity. He assimilates the past in such a way that his life
becomes part of a continuum, yet without the loss of his sense
of his life's uniqueness. This process of revivifying and internal-
izing what in a historical sense is the past becomes in a Christian philosophical sense, his Christian presence.

The river functions most simply as a chronological representation, a progressive tracking of the origins of Christianity in
Britain to the poet's own time. But more importantly, it count-
ers time, transcending the notion of a linear relationship between time and space, dissolving the conceptual boundaries
of past, present, and future. This process facilitates the merger
of self and other over all time toward a unity in Christ.

Nature. As a river image, the Holy River grounds the series
and the poet's view of Christianity in nature. An institution
that may appear to many as antithetical to the natural world is
incorporated untraumatically into the Wordsworthian landscape. The interpenetration of nature and the Church is evidenced in the origin of the series itself, the selection of a site
for a church at Beaumont's Coleorton estate.

Through both narrative and imagery, so pervasive as to be
found to some degree in most of the 132 sonnets, the series
achieves an interpenetration of nature and the Church, exquisitely initiated with the image of the Holy River. On the
simplest level, the river and its banks provide the stage, the
natural world where the human drama unfolds. But the interaction of humanity and the natural world becomes a dynamic
that shapes existence and meaning. The spiritual world is
added to this dynamic when Wordsworth alludes in the second
sonnet to the blood of Christ as a river, his life flowing toward
crucifixion and resurrection, not only for himself, but for all.
The river image then unites the natural world with the spiritual

world and humanity with faith—an interplay not limited to this search for the Holy River, but evidenced throughout Wordsworth's works.

The interpenetration of nature and the Church is an important aspect of a comprehensive understanding of Wordsworth's works because according to this concept, both nature and the Church serve as intermediaries between humanity and God. Within the characteristically Wordsworthian context of God, nature, and humanity, the series focuses on the Church as a manifestation of humanity's striving toward the divine, as nature serves, for the most part throughout his works, as the symbol of the divine covenant with humanity. As nature is the institution of God, so too is the Church the institution of humanity. Nature is deified and the Church naturalized. Humanity, participating in the perpetual dynamic, fulfills its duty—faith; God fulfills the covenant—grace.

Beneath the surface of this scholarly historical versification of British history, then, lies an invaluable insight into Wordsworth's continued attempt to integrate God, nature, and humanity throughout time. The *Ecclesiastical Sonnets* mobilize the integration of a "new" element into the familiar Wordsworthian philosophical landscape, even though churches and church graveyards are unobtrusively present even in his early works.

Theological context of water imagery. Closely related to the interpenetration of nature and the Church initiated by the image of the Holy River is the theological and biblical context that arises from the pervasive water imagery, both literal and figurative. The Holy River begins an evolution of water imagery that culminates in a biblical progression starting with the Flood, with its implications of punishment and purification, to the blood and tears of the Crucifixion, through to baptism and salvation. Water, the lifeblood of nature and all life, merges with the lifeblood of Christ, then through baptism back through water and faith to salvation. Water imagery fuses nature and the Church so intimately that no distinct dichotomy can assert itself: water, the lifeblood of nature, is yoked structurally and symbolically to the blood of Christ, wedding nature to salvation in an eternal bond.

The profusion of water imagery unifies the work, while closely related or repeated water images afford subtle coherence between sonnets, and on occasion to groups of sonnets. Sometimes a word such as *brook* will be repeated as different parts of speech (for example, as a verb in I.20 and as a noun in I.22). Sometimes one use of water imagery will be literal and a nearby one figurative ("Thames to Tyne," I.31; "profaneness flow," I.33; "current of their arms," I.34; "midland brine," I.35). Or in proximate sonnets, water images may be progressive ("brooks" [verb], and "Rhone" in II.11; "rivers," "springs," "fens," "marshes," "Po," and "fountains" in II.13; "floods" and "sea girt Isle" in II.14; "Fleet" and "seas" in II.15; "blood," "tears," and "draught" in II.16; and "brook" [noun], "Streams," "Brook" [noun], "Avon," "Severn," "seas," and "Ocean" in II.17). Fittingly, these examples appear in the group of sonnets on the Protestant rebellion against transubstantiation. This group of sonnets covers the period from Peter Waldo's influence in the twelfth century to the disinterment in 1428 of Wycliffe's bones and their dispersal into a nearby brook, which flows into the sea. This dispersal is represented in sonnet II.17 as the diffusion of Protestant doctrine.

The Purpose of the Series

The purpose of the *Ecclesiastical Sonnets* as stated in the introductory sonnet is "to seek upon the heights of Time the source / Of a HOLY RIVER" (I.1). But the search for origins is abandoned by the fifth sonnet because of the lack of available evidence. The introductory sonnet implies and the beginning sonnets substantiate an objective that is crucial to a viable reading of the series. The work manifests the process of the poet's personal endeavor to come to terms with his own Christian identity, which is inextricably linked to an internalization of the communal Christian past so as to be reconciled with the collective experience of struggle with faith, service, and folly in the fallen world. This process is simultaneously recommended to the reader as a model undertaking. The history of the Church, so ostensibly external and other, so much a series of biographies of famous and unremembered people, interpen-

etrates the history of self just as the life, death, and resurrection of Christ becomes the personal history of each Christian.

The ostensible purpose of the series, to trace the origin and
course of Christianity in Britain, is substantiated by three
pieces of evidence: the prefatory letter, the title of Part I, and
the Fenwick note. The prefatory letter to the *Ecclesiastical
Sonnets* states that after the poet helped George Beaumont
select a site for a church at Coleorton, "it struck [him] that
certain points in the Ecclesiastical History of our Country
might advantageously be presented to view in verse." The title
of Part I reads, "From the Introduction of Christianity into
Britain to the Consummation of the Papal Dominion." The
Fenwick note claims: "My purpose in writing the Series was,
as much as possible, to confine my view to the introduction,
progress, and operation of the Church in England, both previous and subsequent to the Reformation."

But if the poem is read without reference to the prose, the
purpose of the series, in addition to its broad objective and
comprehensive tracing of two thousand years of Christian history in Britain, becomes subtle and personal, and yet operates
in an objective mode by its urging of the process as a model
undertaking for the reader.

The personal nature of the quest is foreshadowed in the
introductory sonnet itself by the repetition of "I," which is also
the first word of the series: "I, who accompanied with faithful
pace / Cerulean Duddon from its cloud-fed spring" and "I,
who essayed the nobler Stream to trace / Of Liberty." This
approach merges the history of the poet, who now seeks the
source of a Holy River, with the history of Christianity.

Although there are only three overtly autobiographical sonnets in this series of 132 (I.22, III.1, and III.22), the importance of the personal role of the poet in the narrative is asserted
from the start and affirmed throughout. The history of Christianity will be filtered through the poet; he will be the measure
of nearly two thousand years of human drama sometimes illu-
minated by and sometimes shaded from divine light. His tracing of the course of history is necessarily selective and unavoidably subjective. But this selection and treatment of topics is

as instructive and thought-provoking as the historical, religious, and political material itself.

The role of the poet culminates in the last sonnet, in which the Word of Christ merges with the word of the poet, the poet as Christian speaking from a divinity that he shares with Christ—now the poet as prophet.

Although the nature of the process is personal, taking its color from the "I," the process of search and discovery is offered at the close of the introductory sonnet as a model to the reader: "for delight of him who tracks its course, / Immortal amaranth and palms abound." As the poet internalizes the past and comes to terms not only with the communal Christian past but with his own Christian identity, the reader is invited to internalize the process and reap the rewards of the "him," which invites a merging of the poet with the reader. The process asserts that while history is the interaction and accumulation of individual lives, the understanding and internalization of history is just as individual and personal.

This process is not a reduction to mere subjectivity, but a recognition of the fundamental role of the individual in the shaping of the future. The rewards promised in the introductory sonnet point to the final sonnet, which addresses the future:

> Why sleeps the future, as a snake enrolled,
> Coil within coil, at noon-tide?
>
> (III.47)

And,

> The living Waters, less and less by guilt
> Stained and polluted, brighten as they roll,
> Till they have reached the eternal City—built
> For the perféct Spirits of the just!
>
> (III.47)

In the first reference, the future is not void but extant, coiled with potential, which can be tapped, according to the poet, by an exploration of the Word approached with imagination, humility, and faith. It is this exploration that becomes the duty of the individual in the present. The poet's vision of the future, with the living waters brightening as they roll, less and less stained and polluted by guilt, is a possible outcome of the fulfilled duty of the individual in the present. This sense of duty arises from engaging in the process demonstrated by the series itself: the poet embarks on a journey in which he revivifies the past, internalizes it, and creates a personal context for it; in the process he comes to terms with the institutionalization of belief and his own faith and identity as a Christian. This intensely personal journey is also universal; it is a process of integrating the self with the past and the future so as to evolve a meaningful present. The poet recommends the process as a model to the reader who is ready to come to a more comprehensive view of the relationship of self to other—living, dead, and yet to be. In this expansive context, a new identity emerges with an inspired and aspiring sense of connection, responsibility, and energy. A future shaped from this stance has indeed the potential to brighten as it rolls.

Simply, then, the series manifests a model process of self-motivated edification, involving a struggle toward broad-based consciousness and an attitude of affirmation capable of affecting the future of the world.

Poet, Text, and Reader

One aspect of the interdynamic among these three elements, the poet, the text, and the reader, lies in the poet's offering his journey toward integration as a model for the reader, who, moved both by the intellectual vigor of the content and the beauty of the poetic text, may identify with the poet so far as to embark on his own search to come to terms with the past, present, and future. The representative character of the journey is reinforced by the poet's seeking "the source / Of a HOLY RIVER," suggesting perhaps that each person has his or her own river to trace to God, with the natural world and, for Christians united in the body of Christ, the Church serving as intermediaries.

Another aspect of the reader's relationship to the material

is modeled in the introductory sonnet by the poet's recognition that coming to terms with the past requires facing distasteful and shameful truths. The flowers and laurels found on the banks of the Holy River have often "crowned . . . the unworthy brow of lawless force." The Church is liable to err, like everything else in the fallen world. The poet carries this critical attitude throughout the series, revealing and attacking injustice and cruelty at times motivated by perverted religious notions. The poet asks the reader to see as clearly as possible by knowing as much as possible.[3] But knowledge itself is not enough. The scathing attack on the Roman Church that ends Part I is followed by the compassionate sanity of the beginning of Part II:

> He only judges right who weighs, compares
> And, in the sternest sentence which his voice
> Pronounces, ne'er abandons Charity.
>
> (II.1)

In fact, this informed, balanced stance is launched in the first sonnet of Part I, which concludes by following the lines criticizing zealous violence with the promise of rewards for anyone willing to seek a comprehensive understanding of the history, to return to first principles by

> seek[ing] upon the heights of Time the source
> Of a HOLY RIVER, on whose banks are found
> Sweet pastoral flowers, and laurels that have crowned
> Full oft the unworthy brow of lawless force;
> And, for delight of him who tracks its course,
> Immortal amaranth and palms abound.

The rewards themselves, however, reflect a bittersweet quality. The permanent red pigment extracted from the leaves and stems of the genus *Amaranthus* is bloodlike; the lasting color and shape of the amaranth flower (either the globe amaranth or the cockscomb) are contingent upon its being dead and dried. The palms recall Christ's triumphant entry into Jerusalem and his subsequent Crucifixion. The poet's subtle but honest reference, at the beginning of the journey, to the ambivalent character of the rewards attempts to prepare the reader for the fact that a Christian's coming to terms with the communal past and his or her own Christian identity is intellectually, psychologically, and spiritually stressful.

But the amaranth does last, and the palms do signify, though dearly purchased, an ultimate and potentially universal victory. And the Holy River itself affords a cooling draught, literally (or figuratively through baptism), along the way to those weary from the journey.

The Structure of the Series Prefigured

Therefore, the introductory sonnet prefigures the structure of the series in three ways. First, the Holy River, as a touchstone of the natural world, as a metaphor for the journey through time, and as a religious symbol, unifies the work around an organic core. It also serves as a foundation for other water imagery that in its profuseness reinforces the coherence of the whole.

Second, the scope of time addressed by the work, and prefigured by the introductory sonnet, is open-ended, covering the uncertain origins of Christianity in Britain to some unknown time in the future, when the last reader of the series rejects the quest or the apocalypse arrives, whichever comes first. This scope of time is understated in the prose attachments and may be viewed as understated in the title of Part III, "From the Restoration to the Present Times," if the reader assumes it refers only to the poet's era.

Third, while the introductory sonnet establishes the poet's personal approach to the history, it prefigures the transformation of the personal into the universal that occurs over the course of the series. The poet, the "I" who has traced the courses of other rivers and now traces the source of a Holy River, serves as a forerunner on this journey and extends his informed critical analysis of events and his balanced judgment as a model to the reader, "him," who is encouraged to take up the quest for himself. This structural process reinforces the use of the Holy River as a unifying element and is reinforced by the expanded amount of time addressed by the work.

Introductory Sonnet I.2

The second sonnet helps to orient the reader to the series by demonstrating key ways in which the work, with 132 sonnets addressing two thousand years of history, achieves meaning and coherence. Most importantly, this sonnet implements the process by which nonlinear concepts of time and water imagery become integral to the work's purpose. The sonnet also begins the first sonnet set, which is a structural technique that sustains coherence within the series. Chapter 3 examines the role of sonnet I.2 in the first sonnet set.

When the first sonnet states that the poet will "seek upon the heights of Time the source / Of a HOLY RIVER," the "heights" of time within the context of the first sonnet seem to refer to significant events in human history related to the origin of Christianity in Britain; the second sonnet then offers three conjectures about sources: St. Paul, St. Peter, or Joseph of Arimathea ("some of humbler name"). But while maintaining this narrative continuity and logic, the second sonnet begins to undermine expectations with its skewed relationship between prophets and the past, and the reader is introduced to the ongoing tension in the work between linear and nonlinear conceptions of time. Time begins to be stripped of its irreversibility and linearity, and it begins to evolve into an amorphous, boundaryless psychological time, which gradually dominates historical time within the work.

> If there be prophets on whose spirits rest
> Past things, revealed like future, they can tell
> What Powers, presiding o'er the sacred well
> Of Christian Faith, this savage Island blessed
> With its first bounty. Wandering through the west,
> Did holy Paul a while in Britain dwell,
> And call the Fountain forth by miracle,
> And with dread signs the nascent Stream invest?
> Or He, whose bonds dropped off, whose prison doors
> Flew open, by an Angel's voice unbarred?
> Or some of humbler name, to these wild shores
> Storm-driven; who, having seen the cup of woe
> Pass from their Master, sojourned here to guard
> The precious Current they had taught to flow?

The sonnet opens with a fusion of past and future, achieved by reversing the conventional role of the prophet from foretelling the future to revealing the past. In a process of synthesis that collapses customary distinctions, the prophet becomes historian, and the past becomes as full of potential as the future. This process of synthesis becomes characteristic of the work and begins in the first sonnet with a fairly traditional merging of poet and historian, a merging of poet and reader, and a merging of the natural and spiritual worlds in the image of the Holy River. The process of synthesis is such that by the last sonnet, the poet as prophet foretells the future, and the period addressed by the work breaks the bounds of time and extends potentially beyond the apocalypse. The work's defiance and manipulation of time has biblical origins, for when Peter warns those who scoff at what seems to them the delay of the Second Coming, he says:

> But, beloved, be not ignorant of this one thing, that one day is with the Lord as a thousand years, and a thousand years as one day. The Lord is not slack concerning his promise, as some men count slackness; but is longsuffering to us-ward, not willing that any should perish, but that all should come to repentance. But the day of the Lord will come as a thief in the night; in which the heavens shall pass away with a great noise, and the elements shall melt with fervent heat; the earth also, and the works that are therein, shall be burned up. (2 Peter 3:8–10)

By applying the role of prophet to the past, the status of the future is conferred on the past, with past and future similarly unknowable, potential, and intriguing. In this process, the past, retrieved from death and completion, is quickened and demands to be experienced as present before it can be known. The work consistently enacts this vivification of the past by the poet's attitude of discovery and participation and the use of verbs in the present tense. These verbs often appear as imperatives and begin the sonnets, as in "Lament!" (I.6), "Watch, and be firm!" (I.8), and "Rise!" (I.10). These and other exclamations, particularly at the beginning of sonnets, contribute to the sense of immediacy of the material: "Enough!" (II.11),

"Praised be the Rivers!" (II.13), "Mother!" (II.25), "Deep is the lamentation!" (II.27), "Woman!" (III.27), and "Glory to God!" (III.46). (Appendix A provides a more complete list of imperatives and exclamations.) While challenging the irreversible nature of linear time, the poet intensifies the experience of the moment, which need never be lost to the past but can be suspended eternally in the present and necessarily in the presence of a reader. The achievement requires a time-lapsed cooperative effort of imagination between reader and poet through the medium of the written word.

Aside from establishing a redefinition of time as integral to the work's purpose, the second sonnet continues the evolution of water imagery begun in sonnet I.1 with the progression of rivers from real to symbolic (Duddon, Liberty, and Holy River). "Sacred well," "Fountain," "Stream," "Storm-driven," "cup of woe," and "precious Current . . . flow" continue the interpenetration of the natural and spiritual worlds, where water and Christianity, and nature and the Church are inextricably linked.

The first three images, the "sacred well," "Fountain," and "Stream" of Christianity, are compatible with the use of the Holy River, the course of Christianity, as a river image. "Storm-driven" functions both literally and figuratively: the first Christians going to Britain undoubtedly faced dangers on stormy seas, but they also were driven by the storms of persecution, a theme carried through sonnets I.3 and I.4 to sonnet I.6, "Persecution."

The last two references, "cup of woe" and "precious Current," are thematically related to persecution and exemplify the complex transmutation of the water imagery. While the water imagery begins with a river image, the Holy River broadly symbolizing the course of Christianity in the natural world, by the end of the second sonnet, the water imagery is modulated, heightened, and refined so as to incorporate the wine of the Last Supper and communion; the blood of the Crucifixion, persecutions, and mortality in general; and the water of baptism, the basis of both biological and eternal life, all flowing into a "precious Current" of faith. This "precious Current" of the Holy River includes the blood of Christ, the

gathering of his faithful followers, and the blood of the perse-
cuted faithful. This complex layering interpenetrates the lifeblood of Christ with the lifeblood of humanity and the lifeblood
of the natural world, uniting all through baptism, which in
conjunction with faith, helps to transcend the earthly struggle.

The merging of these images of blood and water recalls the
First Epistle of John:

> This is he that came by water and blood, even Jesus Christ; not
> by water only, but by water and blood. And it is the Spirit that
> beareth witness, because the Spirit is truth. For there are three
> that bear record in heaven, the Father, the Word, and the Holy
> Ghost: and these three are one. And there are three that bear
> witness in earth, the Spirit, and the water, and the blood: and
> these three agree in one. (5:6–8)

This passage prefaces the coalescence, in the series' final sonnet, of the poetic word with the Word.

The transmutations of water imagery in the second sonnet
anticipate the complex role of the Holy River, which merges
phenomenal and spiritual experience, interpenetrating the
concepts of nature and Christianity. God, made manifest in
Christ, is the source of the Holy River; through the body of
Christ, crucified and resurrected, the river of faith and salvation flows as blood; through the blood of Christ, manifest in
the Word and faith, humanity achieves spiritual immortality,
reflected in the eternal coursing of the river.

The river, then, as a correlative to life, incorporates a stage
of death, which is not only transcended but integral to transcendence. This inherent flux within the eternality of life is
symbolically represented in the relentless birth and death of
the moment in the eternal course of time. On a superficial
level, the work accepts historical time, but only to challenge
it. The work's treatment of material, especially the poet's
involvement, emphasizes both the timeless nature of human
experience and the reader's participation in this continuum.
The "presence" of the past asserts itself in the poetic form itself,
as the poetry transcends the death of its creator, bestowing
immortality on the imagination.

3

The Sonnet Set and Coherence
Within the Series:
Sonnets I.3 to I.5

Small groups of sonnets unified by one or more textual elements help to sustain coherence in this series of 132 sonnets, which are divided into only three extensive parts of thirty-nine, forty-six, and forty-seven sonnets. The title of each part offers only broad chronological guidance ("From the Introduction of Christianity into Britain to the Consummation of the Papal Dominion," "To the Close of the Troubles in the Reign of Charles I," and "From the Restoration to the Present Times"), and there are no subtitles. The sonnets are numbered sequentially within each part and most sonnets have titles, but the titles are typically only one to three words, a brevity that provides at best a sketchy sense of narrative or thematic continuity. Some titles reveal a more direct relationship between sonnets, but not necessarily more specificity, as in sonnet I.19, "Primitive Saxon Clergy" and sonnet I.20, "Other influences"; or as in sonnet II.21, "Dissolution of the monasteries," sonnet II.22, "The same subject," and sonnet II.23, "Continued."

While the sonnets are left to flow freely, uninterrupted by obtrusive subdivisions within the three-part structure, coherence emerges through a network of sonnet sets, in which a particular textual element connects a sonnet not only with the one before and immediately after, but also with several subsequent sonnets. These sonnets may be linked by an aspect of narrative, theme, imagery, or language, and importantly, one set may overlap the boundaries of another. For example, while the fifth sonnet resolves a narrative issue (the acceptance of the uncertainty about the origins of Christianity in Britain) conceived in the first (the quest for the source of the Holy River), the persecution theme and the storm imagery (both begun in sonnet I.2) extend beyond the narrative grouping of sonnets I.2 to I.5 into sonnets I.6 and I.7, while sonnets I.6 to I.13 are unified by the topic of addressing the difficulties inherent in establishing the early Church. These ambiguous beginnings and endings of sonnet sets create overlapping strands of coherence that reinforce the unity of the whole.

In addition, coherence is strengthened by an interweaving of textual elements within and beyond the sonnet sets. These elements, interwoven by juxtaposition or repetition and sometimes in a modified form or a different context, begin to influence one another and set the text resonating on a wealth of biblical, historical, and intratextual associations. For example, while the topic of persecution begins in sonnet I.2 with Peter and leads to Alban's martyrdom in sonnet I.6, both references recall the Crucifixion of Christ, especially in Peter's choosing to be crucified head downward because he deemed himself unworthy to die in the same manner as his Savior. Sonnet I.8, "Temptations from Roman refinements," confirms this thread of association, linking sonnets I.2 through I.8, with a direct reference to Christ's Crucifixion.

Another example involves the repetition of a word, used sometimes literally and sometimes figuratively. When the word is used literally, it resonates with the nearby figurative meaning and sets up intriguing tensions with related textual elements. In sonnet I.2, for instance, the word "storm" projects through to sonnet I.7 with "Storm-driven" (I.2), "coming storm" (I.4), "storm hath ceased" (I.7), and "survivors of this Storm" (I.7). The crossing of stormy seas merging with storms of persecution instigates a process of interaction between water imagery and thematic elements of persecution such that "cup of woe" and "precious Current" in sonnet I.2 elicit associations that evolve through the seven subsequent sonnets and lead to the metamorphosis of sea water into the blood of Christ in sonnet I.8:

> Your love of Him upon whose forehead sate
> The crown of thorns; whose life-blood flowed, the price
> Of your redemption.

This interweaving of textual elements within and between sonnets, between sonnet sets, and between the text and external sources creates a pattern of association that evolves ideas integral to the series' purpose; this interweaving of textual elements underscores the work's artistry and imbues the series with the embellished texture of an intricately embroidered tapestry.[1]

This chapter examines the first sonnet set, sonnets I.1 to I.5, as an example of the use of sonnet sets in the series and offers a close reading of sonnets I.3 to I.5, the first two sonnets having been discussed in the previous chapter. As the first set, it introduces the work's organic structure, revealing the interaction of textual elements, the relationship between sonnets, and the role of the individual sonnet in relation to the whole. This first set also introduces important aspects of the work's character: the poet's creative use of extensive historical research, his challenging of conventional concepts of time, and his reaffirmation of a synthetic worldview, manifested here on a large scale as a merging of nature and Christianity. The following discussion takes its shape from the thorough interfacing of narrative and theme in this set, the treatment of time reinforced by a particular use of language, and the role of imagery in treating both landscape and meaning.

To briefly review the narrative of this sonnet set, sonnet I.1, "Introduction," establishes the quest for the source of the Holy River; sonnet I.2, "Conjectures," speculates about the origin of Christianity in Britain; sonnet I.3, "Trepidation of the Druids," suddenly regresses in time to foreshadow the impending ruin of pagan dominance and the conversion of the druids to Christianity; and sonnet I.4, "Druidic excommunication," offers an intriguing presentation of the druids as a medium, albeit fallen and corrupted, for the "primal truth" (I.4) that infused the world at its creation. This "primal truth," which recognizes the source of all in God, readies the acceptance in sonnet I.5, "Uncertainty," that the origin of Christianity in Britain remains a mystery and that it is enough to see the evidence of its early and continuing presence. Accepting the mystery about origins may seem to be an act of complacency, but it presages the intellectual and spiritual leap necessary for faith itself. The narrative, with its evolving philosophical implications, casts a shadow back over the "we are lost" in the first line of sonnet I.5.

The topic of reward, introduced in sonnet I.1, for seekers of the source of the Holy River, is starkly juxtaposed with the persecution experienced by those who are conjectured in sonnet I.2 to have been the source of Christianity in Britain. The theme of persecution comes to dominate this set and indeed radiates beyond it into sonnets I.6 and I.7. The thematic set, sonnets I.2 to I.7, thus overlaps the narrative set, sonnets I.1 to I.5. While sonnet I.2 begins to draw attention to the topics of the Crucifixion, persecution, and the spreading faith (through reference to Peter's imprisonment, and by implication, his subsequent crucifixion, and the use of "Storm-driven," "cup of woe," and "precious Current [of faith]"), sonnet I.3 brings these elements to the fore:

> —the Julian spear
> A way first opened; and, with Roman chains,
> The tidings come of Jesus crucified;
> They come—they spread—the weak, the suffering, hear;
> Receive the faith, and in the hope abide.

The "Julian spear" refers to the Roman conquest of Gaul, which carried the news of Christianity to Britain,[2] but the image also calls up the piercing of Christ's side at the Crucifixion. The image merges the theme of persecution with the Crucifixion, collapsing time and making immediate "the tidings . . . of Jesus crucified."

Sonnet I.4, "Druidical excommunication," addresses an early Briton who faces persecution (cut off from warmth, food, and human sympathy) because he or she has been touched by Christianity:

> Mercy and Love have met thee on thy road,
> Thou wretched Outcast, from the gift of fire
> And food cut off by sacerdotal ire,
> From every sympathy that Man bestowed!

The theme of persecution, begun in sonnet I.2, carried through to sonnet I.3, and temporarily resolved in sonnets I.6 and I.7, refers to Roman oppression. The persecution in sonnet I.4, however, is by the druids, who themselves led rebellions against the Romans. But the sonnet points out that despite the druidic persecution of this "Outcast," who might be an early Christian, the druids (according to Wordsworth's view of them) believed in God as the sole source of wisdom, justice, and order:

> Yet shall it claim our reverence, that to God,
> Ancient of days! that to the eternal Sire,
> These jealous Ministers of law aspire,
> As to the one sole fount whence wisdom flowed,
> Justice, and order.
>
> (I.4)

This sense of God infused the world at its creation, perhaps presaging future religious struggles:

> Tremblingly escaped,
> As if with prescience of the coming storm,
> *That* intimation when the stars were shaped.
>
> (I.4)

And even during the period of paganism, a certain sense of this monotheism prevailed (the poet uses present tense), even though one may vainly grieve at the forms it took:

> And still, 'mid yon thick woods, the primal truth
> Glimmers through many a superstitious form
> That fills the Soul with unavailing ruth.
>
> (I.4)

Sonnet I.5, "Uncertainty," takes up the three themes subtly, with concluding lines that emphasize the spreading faith. An-

cient ruins, monuments, ancient poetry, and Greek and Roman history and myth create a cumulative context that tells an
ongoing tale of suffering:

> Darkness surrounds us; seeking, we are lost
> On Snowdon's wilds, amid Brigantian coves,
> Or where the solitary shepherd roves
> Along the plain of Sarum, by the ghost
> Of Time and shadows of Tradition, crost;
> And where the boatman of the Western Isles
> Slackens his course—to mark those holy piles
> Which yet survive on bleak Iona's coast.
> Nor these, nor monuments of eldest name,
> Nor Taliesin's unforgotten lays,
> Nor characters of Greek or Roman fame,
> To an unquestionable Source have led;
> Enough—if eyes, that sought the fountain-head
> In vain, upon the growing Rill may gaze.

The "plain of Sarum" (and Stonehenge), justifiably or not,
calls up sacrifices, human or otherwise, which connect suffering to persecutions. The "growing Rill" refers to the spread of
the faith in Britain, the evidence of which at that early time
(second to third centuries) is unfortunately manifested in the
persecution of the faithful, as shown in sonnet I.6. But in the
extended view, the growing Rill becomes the Holy River, the
"living Waters [that] brighten as they roll [toward] the eternal
City."

The work's characteristic disregard for conventional concepts of time begins in the second sonnet with the peculiar
but still fairly reasonable speculation that the origin of Christianity in Britain could be discovered if the power of prophets
extended back in time as well as forward. But the seemingly
innocuous space between the second and third sonnets hurls
the reader and the poet centuries back in time to where they
stand witnessing druids auguring the future, which had
seemed, a psychic instant ago, the ancient past:

> Screams round the Arch-druid's brow the sea-mew—white
> As Menai's foam; and toward the mystic ring
> Where Augurs stand, the Future questioning,
> Slowly the cormorant aims her heavy flight,

Portending ruin to each baleful rite
That, in the lapse of ages, hath crept o'er
Diluvian truths, and patriarchal lore.
Haughty the Bard: can these meek doctrines blight
His transports? wither his heroic strains?
But all shall be fulfilled;—the Julian spear
A way first opened; and, with Roman chains,
The tidings come of Jesus crucified;
They come—they spread—the weak, the suffering, hear;
Receive the faith, and in the hope abide.

                                                          (I.3)

Immediacy breathes through the series, achieved in part by
the use of verbs in the present tense, with sonnet I.3 offering
an especially effective use. The sonnet opens with inverted
word order, so that the first word of the sonnet is "screams."
There is no delay; the first word intensifies the immediacy of
the scene and jars the reader as the sound itself must have
alarmed the druid. In one word, the poet conjures a time warp
and a radical shift in perspective.

Nothing so chronologically drastic occurs in the next sonnet
or again in the series until the conclusion, which propels
the work, poet, and reader into the apocalyptic future. Time
touches sonnet I.4 subtly in that the "primal truth" of God as
"the one sole fount" of "wisdom, . . . / Justice and order," a
consciousness created with the stars at the beginning of the
world, "Glimmers" throughout time—even through the druidic pagan rites.

Sonnet I.5, which accepts that the origin of Christianity in
Britain remains a mystery, provides the series' first detailed
symbolic landscape that gives a sense of closure to the arresting
time/space disjuncture discharged without warning in sonnet
I.3. This visual image, though somewhat threatening in content, affords some comfort in the familiarity of its natural
elements.

Darkness surrounds us; seeking, we are lost
On Snowdon's wilds, amid Brigantian coves,
Or where the solitary shepherd roves
Along the plain of Sarum, by the ghost

> Of Time and shadows of Tradition, crost;
> And where the boatman of the Western Isles
> Slackens his course—to mark those holy piles
> Which yet survive on bleak Iona's coast.
>   (I.5)

The journey through this early history, even with the discovery of evidence of early Celtic Christianity, has not led to the source of Christianity in Britain.[3] But the evidence of its existence is enough: even if the origin ("fountain-head") of the Holy River remains a mystery, the "growing Rill" is visible. The resolution of the dramatic time/space transformation into a landscape of natural elements (despite the ghost), parallels the resolution to forego the quest for the source of the Holy River and to accept the ultimate origin as God—or perhaps the Holy Ghost.

Nature imagery continues to interweave the historical narrative with the religious theme so that nature and the Church, and water and Christianity, continue as the warp and weft of the series' tapestry. To the water and flower imagery of sonnet I.1 and the water and water-to-wine/blood/faith imagery of sonnet I.2, sonnet I.3 adds the series' first animals: two seabirds, a seagull and a cormorant. Sonnet I.3 continues the water imagery with "Menai's foam" and "Diluvian truths." Sonnet I.4 adds "fire," "stars," and "thick woods" to the nature imagery and continues the water imagery with "fount whence wisdom flowed" and "coming storm." And sonnet I.5 offers the series' first painterly scene with its landscape components of "darkness," "Snowdon's wilds," "Brigantian coves," "solitary shepherd," "plain of Sarum," "boatman of the Western Isles," "holy piles," "bleak Iona's coast," "monuments," "fountain-head," and "growing Rill." While sonnet I.3 offers a powerful, though sketchy, scene with the sea-mew screaming around the brow of the Arch-druid and the cormorant heaving its heavy flight toward the mystic ring where the augurs stand questioning the future, sonnet I.5 offers the first detailed Wordsworthian landscape. Given the multifaceted responsibility of the series' introductory sonnets, it is rather remarkable that the nineteenth-century landscape painting tradition arises in a sonnet as close to the beginning as the fifth.[4]

The birds of sonnet I.3, the light of sonnet I.4, and the darkness of sonnet I.5 introduce significant textural elements of the series' nature pattern. Of the at least thirty-four animal images in the series, a minimum of seventeen are of birds, which is not surprising given the extensive religious symbolism associated with these animals.[5]

In sonnet I.3, the sea-mew, white as the foam on the strait of Menai, screams around the head of the chief druid; and as the druidic priests stand in their mystic circle foretelling the future, the cormorant flies toward them, foreshadowing the end of druidic dominance, which has taken hold in this post-lapsarian world ("lapse of ages," I.3), prone to err, displacing the lessons of the Flood (punishment and purification) and disparaging of God's covenant.[6]

The two birds elicit religious associations because they are seabirds noted for their fishing and because they are placed in a druidic context. They thereby continue the interpenetration of nature and water imagery with Christianity. Furthermore, as birds in flight, serving as messengers to those on the ground, they connect the landscape with the sky in a way that is reminiscent of the use of imagery in "Tintern Abbey." Unification of the landscape and the deepening of its significance is achieved in "Tintern Abbey" with cliffs jutting against the sky and smoke rising in columns from the woods. The landscape is connected to the sky, and humanity is merged subtly into the seclusion: "steep and lofty cliffs . . . connect the landscape with the quiet sky" (5–8) and "wreaths of smoke" from pastoral farms rise "in silence, from among the trees" (18). The birds in sonnet I.3, messengers of Christianity in the context created by the poet, connect the spiritual and natural worlds. As seabirds come inland before a storm, they reappear to celebrate and rebuild their nests in sonnet I.7, "Recovery," after the storm of persecution.

Light and dark imagery figures strongly in the series with a minimum of one hundred references, which recall the emphasis on light and dark imagery in the Bible.[7] The fourth sonnet

introduces light in the form of fire and stars, and the fifth
sonnet introduces darkness with its first word. Light/dark imagery is carried forward in the very next sonnet, with "fiery
sword" and "lightning" and evolves throughout the work in
numerous ways, in references to, for example, sunlight, dawn,
fire, flames, burning, tapers, torch, glowworms, night, mid-
night, shade, shadow, blackness, gloominess, and heavy
clouds. The visual contrast of the cumulative light/dark imagery suggests the spiritual and psychological tension of the
human drama, both in its original enactment and in its recollection, that the work portrays and meditates upon.

4

"For the Word . . . Yields Power": The Role of Language in Sonnets I.6 to I.14

The historical narrative of this sonnet set may pose some difficulty for the reader because it covers three hundred densely textured years from the persecution of the Christians under the reign of Diocletian (284–305) to the evangelical mission of St. Augustine (c. 597). The sonnets address the struggles of the early Church in Britain: the sadistic violence of Roman persecution, the corrupting influence of Roman decadence, the foolish and hate-nurturing heresies, the consigning to the flames of churches and documents, the imprisonment and slaughter of clergy, and for the early Britons in general, the dehumanization of slavery.

This intriguing sonnet set orchestrates a dynamic narrative that recounts the Christian struggle against persecution, oppression, invasions, and mass slaughter, while simultaneously playing on the power of language itself: the ascendancy of the word/Word over violence and cruelty. These sonnets show that language not only offers comfort as a buffer against the tragedy of human existence, but it also empowers, creates, and immortalizes.

The interpenetration of nature and Christianity continues to serve a central structural and symbolic role and is, in fact, an integral part of the language play of this section. Nature and the Church are drawn together by an interfacing of language, music, and poetry. The singing of birds merges with human

hymns of praise and thanksgiving, words chime, harps of the
Welsh bards connect poetry and music with angelic harp music
and the divine Word, and a battle is won by the singing of
"hallelujah" from the mountain tops over the heads of the
invaders. Nature serves actively in a manner befitting the
Wordsworthian tradition: as a significant landscape that offers
a correlative of human experience, as a participant in the
human drama ("melancholy Stream" and "indignant Hills" in
sonnet I.12), and as a palpable reassurance of the divine
presence.

This sonnet set addresses and demonstrates the power of
language and becomes a defense of poetry, memory, and revelation through the word/Word. Poetry links individual memory with the collective human spirit—past, present, and future. The attention to language in this section prepares the
way for the progressive evolution throughout the series of the
merging of the poetic word with the prophetic—a coalescence
completed and powerfully articulated in the final sonnet,
III.47. The preparation for this coalescence, begun in sonnets
I.6 to I.14, is so thorough that the evolution of the versification
of history into the prophesying of the future and of the fusion
of poet and prophet, comes in sonnet III.47 not as a surprise,
but as a logical outgrowth of the organic process of the work.
This process is one of the striking characteristics of the series
that qualifies it for current critical attention and for inclusion
in the Wordsworth canon.

This chapter examines the thematic role of language in the
historical narrative, which relates the powerful role of language
in the course of human—and miraculous—events. It also examines the set's use of language, which demonstrates the
power of the word through inspired use of rhetorical techniques such as juxtaposition, proximitous repetition, quotation, exclamation, and allusion, all of which invite evocative
sets of association. These techniques necessarily overlap, just
as the thematic role of language interfaces with the historical
narrative and the rhetorical use of language. Although language takes on special significance in this set, these sonnets
exemplify the artistry that suffuses the series.

With seventeen overt references, language takes on an im-

portant thematic role in this set of nine sonnets. Language
becomes a topic in the historical narrative as it covers a period
of invasions that cause tension and competition between the
native Celtic language and the language of the invading Romans and Saxons (sonnets I.8 and I.12). Sonnet I.13 draws
particular attention to language by pivoting on wordplay.
There are three references to prayer (sonnets I.9, I.12, and
I.14) and two references to "words" (sonnets I.10 and I.14),
and sonnet I.11 refers to a battle won by three repetitions of
the word "hallelujah." Language is both a positive and negative
force, and surprisingly, in two of the three references to
prayer, of no effect whatsoever.

The first of two negative references to language occurs in
relation to the temptation from Roman refinements in which

> Language, and letters;—these, though fondly viewed
> As humanizing graces, are but parts
> And instruments of deadliest servitude!
>
> (I.8)

The second reference is to the nearly wholesale usurpation of
Britain by the Saxon language and culture, so that

> Another language spreads from coast to coast;
> Only perchance some melancholy Stream
> And some indignant Hills old names preserve,
> When laws, and creeds, and people are all lost!
>
> (I.12)

Reference to the names of places actually begins in the last
sonnet of the previous set with "monuments of eldest name"
(I.5) and carries through this set with four more references.
The first is to Alban's name, which shall not forsake the hill
that absorbed his martyred blood and now decks itself with
flowers in his memory (I.6); the second reference is to the
renaming of places in the new Saxon tongue (I.12). Two more
references occur in sonnet I.13 with Gregory's wordplay on
Angles: "ANGLI by name" ("ANGLI" and "ANGEL"), and "having
learnt that name, salvation craves / For Them." There is also

wordplay on "DE-IRIANS" and "save[d] . . . from God's IRE," and "AELLA" and "HALLE-lujahs."

The reader might expect the work to provide a more favorable treatment of the power of prayer, but when the Britons pray for the Romans to remain to defend them from imminent invasions by the Saxons and Picts, "vain are suppliant cries, / And prayers that would undo her forced farewell" (I.9). Vain also are the supplications of the monks at the monastery of old Bangor whose

> prayers would turn
> The sword from Bangor's walls, and guard the store
> Of Aboriginal and Roman lore.
>
> (I.12)

The monks are slaughtered, the Christian monuments are burned, and the monastery is demolished by Ethelforth and his troops. However, the chanted prayer of St. Augustine and his procession has more favorable results:

> the tempestuous sea
> Of Ignorance, that ran so rough and high
> And heeded not the voice of clashing swords,
> These good men humble by a few bare words,
> And calm with fear of God's divinity.
>
> (I.14)

The "few bare words" succeed where the "clashing swords" do not, and a pattern emerges in conjunction with sonnet I.10 in which words and swords are juxtaposed:

> [Bards] Rush on the fight, to harps preferring swords,
> And everlasting deeds to burning words!

In both sonnets the juxtaposition occurs in the last lines, with each word ending the line, with "words" coming last in each juxtaposition, and with "words" having the last word in sonnet I.10 and the penultimate word in I.14, followed by "divinity."

Unlike the "few bare words" of Augustine, the "burning words" of the Welsh bards remain potential and unmanifested, for the bards have relinquished their harps for swords. Despite the glory of war described in sonnet I.10, and in light of the extent of the Saxon conquest, this sonnet in conjunction with I.14 argues in favor of the dominance of the word over the sword, both in power and duration. The "few bare [but chanted] words" dominate over "Ignorance" and the sword. The sword represents the transience of human existence, while words survive, unifying the human community, living and dead, beyond time.

The most striking example of the poet's juxtaposing the word to the sword is in sonnet I.11, "Saxon conquest," which refers to the Hallelujah Victory, a battle won without bloodshed. Germanus, a monk and formerly a distinguished Roman soldier, orchestrates a victory over the Saxons and Picts by having the Britons shout "hallelujah" from the mountaintops over the heads of the invading army, dispersing them in panic.[1] Victory is achieved by faith and three repetitions of the word "hallelujah."

The juxtaposition of "swords" and "words" demonstrates how the thematic role of language is often inseparable from its rhetorical use as these functions overlap and reinforce each other. For instance, the two juxtapositions of "swords" with "words" (I.10 and I.14) are strategically placed before and after the battle won by the word "hallelujah" (I.13).

Juxtaposition is also used in the rich accumulation of music imagery that not only continues the interpenetration of nature and the Church but links them with language and poetry. An element of nature introduces the musical dimension to the series, and nature continues to play a strong role in this history of the Church, as evidenced by the multitude of relevant images in this set (water in sonnets I.8, I.11, I.12, and I.13; light in sonnets I.6, I.8, and I.10; dark in sonnets I.9 and I.11; burning in sonnets I.6, I.9, I.10, and I.12; flowers in sonnet I.6; field in sonnets I.10 and I.11; wood in sonnets I.8, I.10, and I.11; hills in sonnets I.10, I.11, and I.12; fane in sonnet I.7; Earth, foss, and barrow in sonnet I.11; roots in sonnet I.9; thorns in sonnet I.8; and birds in sonnet I.7). Recalling the sea-mew and cormorant in sonnet I.3, and looking ahead to the sparrow in sonnet I.16, it is not surprising that the introduction of music comes in the form of bird song.

Music is introduced in sonnet I.7 with birds "chant[ing] a congratulating hymn / To the blue ether and bespangled plain" in celebration of their surviving a storm. In the same sonnet, human hymns of praise and thanksgiving are offered by the survivors of the storm of persecution. Music, then, in its very introduction, links nature with faith. Eleven references to music appear thereafter throughout the seven subsequent sonnets of this group, though indirectly in sonnet I.8.

Two references directly relate music to poetry: the "harps" of the Welsh bards in sonnet I.10 and the "song" of Taliesin in sonnet I.12. Six references relate to human voices: "vocal gratitude" in sonnet I.7; "hallelujahs" in sonnet I.11; "song of Taliesin" in sonnet I.12; "chiming sound" in sonnet I.13, referring to the voice of Gregory; "sing / Glad HALLE-lujahs" in sonnet I.13; and "Chanting . . . a tuneful prayer— / Sung for themselves, and those who they would free" in sonnet I.14. There are two references to instruments: "knell" in sonnet I.9 and "harps" in sonnet I.10. The examples draw the voices of animals, humans, and instruments together into a context that resonates on the interplay of nature and human experience joined by a universal language of music.

Another rhetorical device, previously discussed in relation to the first sonnet set and used in this set to highlight the role of language, is proximitous repetition. In the first set, the word "storm" is repeated three times, with plays on its connections to nature imagery and religious persecution. Repetition in this set draws attention to language not only by its frequency, but also by what is repeated. For instance, "name(s)" is repeated five times (in sonnets I.5, I.6, I.12, and twice in sonnet I.13); "prayer(s)" is repeated three times (in sonnets I.9, I.12, and I.14); "sword(s)" is repeated four times (in sonnets I.6, I.10, I.12, and I.14); "words" is repeated twice (in sonnets I.10 and I.14); and "hallelujahs" is repeated twice (in sonnets I.11 and I.13).

The repetitions complement the musical dimension by creating echoes. In the following examples, the echoes undulate with alliteration: Alban's "Hill" (I.6), "hallelujahs tost from hill to hill" (I.11), "indignant Hills" (I.12), and "HALLE-lujahs" (I.13). The reference to the Hallelujah Victory in sonnet I.11

demonstrates the power of the word conjured in its three repetitions by the soldiers and its echoing "from hill to hill." The hallelujahs save the soldiers' lives; when the hallelujahs are repeated in sonnet I.13, they save the Britons' souls.

The use of quotation emphasizes language's role in the continuity and connectedness of the human drama. Language as one medium of memory (individual and collective) transcends the relentless irreversible progressiveness of time.

The first two lines of sonnet I.12 are from Taliesin, a fourteenth-century poet, believed in Wordsworth's time to be a Welsh bard of the sixth century. The lines are not quoted directly; Wordsworth presents them, as if to emphasize memory, with dashes as though he is selectively recalling the phrases that seem to burn the past into the emotional present: *"The oppression of the tumult—wrath and scorn— / The tribulation—and the gleaming blades—"*[2]

Another use of quotation follows this set closely in sonnet I.16, the whole of which is the quoted speech of Paulinus to King Edwin, both introduced in sonnet I.15. The quotation demonstrates the role of language in spreading the faith, for Paulinus' speech converts Edwin and his court to Christianity, indeed moving the court's pagan priest to ride forth in full career

> To desecrate the Fane which heretofore
> He served in folly. Woden falls, and Thor
> Is overturned
> . . . .
> . . . and the God himself is seen no more.
> (I.17)

A quotation follows this description, based on Matthew 11:28: " *'O come to me, / Ye heavy laden!'.'"* The positioning of a quotation from Taliesin in sonnet I.12, one from Paulinus' conversion of the Britons in sonnet I.16, and the words of Christ in sonnet I.17 collects into the same context poetry, history, politics, and religion—a microcosm of the context created by the *Ecclesiastical Sonnets* as a whole.

Regarding the use of quotation throughout the series,

Wordsworth acknowledges extensive debts to historical writers. Wordsworth's note to sonnet I.11 reads:

> The last six lines of the sonnet are chiefly from the prose of Daniel; and here I will state (though to the Readers whom this Poem will chiefly interest it is unnecessary) that my obligations to other prose writers are frequent,—obligations which, even if I had not a pleasure in courting, it would have been presumptuous to shun, in treating an historical subject. I must, however, particularize Fuller, to whom I am indebted in the Sonnet upon Wicliffe and in other instances. And upon the acquittal of the Seven Bishops I have done little more than versify a lively description of that event in the MS. Memoirs of the first Lord Lonsdale.

Wordsworth's extensive research and his incorporation of the work of other writers is evidence of the importance of language in an informed understanding of the past that enriches the present and offers hope to the future.

An introductory imperative exclamation begins this sonnet set and introduces the technique to the series. Exclamations, used about 160 times throughout the series, appear twenty times in first lines, though they are not always imperatives.

In this set, introductory imperative exclamations are used three times in an alternating pattern, in sonnets I.6, I.8, and I.10. This is a rather high density for a group of nine sonnets. Given 132 sonnets and twenty introductory exclamations, the average is about one for every six sonnets. Only in the concluding sonnets of the series (III.42, III.44, and III.46) is this technique used again with such cumulative intensity.

The imperative nature of the exclamations, together with their frequency and strategic placement ("Lament!," "Watch!," "Watch, and be firm!," and "Rise!"), thrust the historical narrative into the present and the reader into the action. This drawing in of the reader is reinforced in sonnet I.8 with the first use in the series of direct address to the reader. "Your" is repeated three times in this sonnet, with the first use clearly addressing the Britons of the historical period; the second and third uses could address the reader as well:

Your love of Him upon whose forehead sate
The crown of thorns; whose life-blood flowed, the price
Of your redemption.

The imperative exclamations and the use of direct address to
the reader dissolve conceptual barriers; the dead are resurrected by addressing them fervently in the present tense,
and Britons of the third and fourth centuries are addressed
simultaneously with the reader, present and future.[3]
    But this rhetorical maneuvering achieves even more far-
reaching effects, for the intensity of the words "Lament!,"
"Watch!," and "Rise!," beyond the importance of their own
contexts, calls forth biblical associations such as the Lamentations of Jeremiah; "Watch ye therefore: for ye know not when
the master . . . cometh. . . . Watch" (Mark 13:35–37), Christ's
raising of the dead (for example, Luke 8:54–55), the Resurrection itself, and the promise of eternal life. These associations
issue from the dynamic interplay of the evocative text and the
anticipated resources of the reader's mind. The associations
are also prompted and nurtured by rhetorical techniques, used
with calculated subtlety for a masterful effect.
    Familiarity with Wordsworth's works encourages a strong
awareness of the value of association. Both the prose and
poetry emphasize the importance of synthetic interrelation-
ships—one person to the community of humankind, the individual to nature, the individual to the Church, the Church to
nature, and nature to God. We see the emphasis in Wordsworth's effort to arrange his works in the collected editions to
highlight their relationship with one another. Allusion and
direct reference are used within a work, and among works, to
set up resonances. The echo of a word, phrase, image, or
theme draws together two different contexts that no longer
achieve meaning solely within themselves.
    The first sonnet of the series provides an obvious example
of the poet's technique. It refers directly to the *Duddon* and
Liberty, and plays indirectly upon the river imagery of *The
Prelude.* This referencing is an invitation to hear echoes, to
refresh the memory, to connect. The technique enriches experience, for the present moment becomes pregnant with both

the past and the future. This stance, for the poet, is what makes a comprehensive, purposive philosophy possible.

The attention to the power of language in this sonnet set evolves ultimately toward the prophetic word, which looks both forward and backward and is manifested in the Word, both biblical and poetic. For in the very beginning there was language: "And God said, Let there be light: and there was light" (Genesis 1:3); "In the beginning was the Word, and the Word was with God, and the Word was God" (John 1:1); and Adam named the beasts (Genesis 2:19–20) and created a relationship between humans and animals that is still being debated. Therefore, Wordsworth portrays, and does not merely assign, the important role of language in the historical narrative.

Twice in this group of sonnets, Wordsworth refers to the burning of words: in I.12, with the destruction of the monastery at Bangor, and in I.10, with the "burning words" of the Welsh bards. Although the poet deplores the destruction of the monastery and its Christian records, the literal burning of the Word is ineffectual against the burning Word that is emblazoned on the memory and the soul and that sheds light through the centuries despite horrendous oppression, cruelty, misinterpretation, zealousness, and other endless forms of human folly.

Attention to the power of the word also evolves into a defense of poetry, for the rhyming of poetry in the oral tradition was in part a mnemonic device—a way to make the word endure, a way that avoids the limits of the written word that could be burned, ignored, or forgotten. In its use of quotations and resonances the work becomes a representative defense of individual memory, collective memory, and consciousness. In fact, difficulties that readers may have with the work may only substantiate the need of such a defense.

5

The Sanctuary of Faith:
Sonnets I.15 to I.25

The narrative of these sonnets covers nearly three hundred years of English Church history from St. Augustine's conversion of Kent in 597 (I.14) to the reign of Alfred (871–899), king of the West Saxons (I.26). The first half of this set focuses on the process of conversion, with four sonnets on or relating to Paulinus' conversion of Northumbria (I.15 to I.18) and one sonnet on missionary activity in general (I.25). The next six sonnets highlight some of the attractions of Christianity: the benefits to the individual and society of even imperfect faith (I.18 and I.24); the salubrious influence of the clergy (I.19); the consolation offered through the rites for the burial of the dead (I.20); inducements of the cloister (I.21 to I.22); and praise of the energetic Bede, Church historian and devoted scholar, whose revered history of the Church has salvation as its principal theme (I.23).

This sonnet set has special significance in terms of helping the reader understand the character and impress of the series as a whole. First, the interpenetration of nature and the Church is emphasized as integral to the organic life of the work—not merely as a decorative motif but at one with the series' purpose. The Church is absorbed into the natural world, the Church takes nature into itself, and nature serves, for the first time in the series, as an intermediary between the body and the soul. Second, the poet becomes a character in the narrative, revealing the personalization of the Church history. Third, the poet's treatment of fancy and the supernatural in religion offers intriguing evidence against critics' assertions about the onset of the poet's deathlike state of orthodoxy. Fourth, the poet's Idea of the Church and its role in his synthetic worldview emerges with clarity in the rarefied atmosphere created by the cumulative effect of the first three significant aspects of this set of sonnets.

The Church Merges with the Natural World

While the subject of the series is Church history, its content manifests itself overwhelmingly in images of the natural world. In this set of eleven sonnets, for instance, there are about thirty-five references to animals, trees, water, vegetation, and weather.[1] More significant than the sheer number of images is the poet's linking of the soul to nature through a sparrow and of the voice of Christ to the voice of streams. Nature becomes an intermediary between the body and the soul, and a metaphor for faith—as in the larger Wordsworthian context, nature is a metaphor for all meaning, which is ultimately founded on faith. The Church takes nature into itself while it is also absorbed into the natural context as an institution, architectural element, and symbol of humanity's striving toward the divine.

The interpenetration process transcends the use of imagery as a mere embellishment to the narration. Instead, the narrative merges with its imagery so that the metaphors link humanity to God through nature. The most striking examples occur in sonnets I.16, I.17, and I.21.

Sonnet I.16 alludes to a well-known passage in Bede, in which the flight of a sparrow from the winter's cold into the warmth of the firelit room symbolizes the transience of the soul's visitation in the body.[2] In sonnet I.17, the voice of Christ "heard near fresh streams," in the context of a call to baptism and faith in " 'O come to me, / Ye heavy laden!',", becomes associated with and merges with the voice of streams themselves. This is another example of the impress of resonances in the poet's works,[3] for the reader familiar with the works cannot help but associate this passage with the ascent of Snowdon in the final book of *The Prelude* in which the poet witnesses the "mount[ing] . . . roar of waters, torrents, streams / Innumerable, roaring with one voice" (1805.XIII.58–59); this vision is then associated with

> a mighty Mind,
> . . . that feeds upon infinity,
> That is exalted by an underpresence,
> The sense of God.[4]
>
>   (1805.XIII:69–72)

The third notable example of a merging through metaphor occurs in sonnet I.21, "Seclusion," in which "the war-worn Chieftain quits the world" and enters a monastery, not for rest but for spiritual labor. His experience is described with images that merge humanity's being, mental life, and spiritual presence with nature:

> Within his cell,
> Round the decaying trunk of human pride,
> At morn, and eve, and midnight's silent hour,
> Do penitential cogitations cling;
> Like ivy, round some ancient elm, they twine
> In grisly folds and strictures serpentine;
> Yet, while they strangle, a fair growth they bring,
> For recompense—their own perennial bower.

Other mergings through metaphor of nature and humanity occur in sonnets I.14, I.15, I.19, and I.24. Similar to the above example, sonnet I.19 compares the primitive Saxon clergy to trees:

> How beautiful your presence
> · · · · · · · · · · · ·
> . . . who, outwardly as bare
> As winter trees, yield no fallacious sign
> That the firm soul is clothed with fruit divine!

In sonnet I.15, St. Paulinus' nose is referred to as an "eagle's beak." In sonnet I.24, the people, busily building a church, are playfully compared to "congregated bees." In sonnet I.14, pagan Britain is portrayed as "the tempestuous sea / Of Ignorance."

The mergers in sonnets I.14 to I.17, I.19, I.21, and I.24 involve an interpenetration of nature and the Church through a human medium. The merger in sonnet I.22 differs slightly in that an element of nature is bound directly with an element of the Church: "nor should e'er the crested fowl . . . his matins sing for me." In all eight of these examples, while the subject of the narrative is the Church, the content is articulated through images of the natural world.

The message, then, transcends Church history. The series is indeed a history of the Church, but it is a personalized Wordsworthian history in which the Church is a manifestation of the natural world. Wordsworth's vision synthesizes, whereas Western intellectual tradition tends to compartmentalize. His vision transcends the notion of humanity against nature, nature against the Church, or humanity against God (or vice versa). Wordsworth's vision is harmonic, but certainly not blind to inevitable periodic discordances. His vision is Edenistic without being naive. There is a clear and persistent sense that indicates a return to a state of spiritual, intellectual, and societal purity reminiscent of the prelapsarian world, but richer, more philosophical, and more meaningful because of the consciousness of the return through spiritual striving and especially through grace. This is the nature of the apocalyptic vision at the end of the series: "The living Waters, less and less by guilt / Stained and polluted, brighten as they roll" (III.47).

It is not a vision of postapocalyptic salvation, because that for Wordsworth would posit a suicidal God: Wordsworth's God loves the Earth and the natural world too much to destroy it. This is not an issue of God's limitations, as if God could not exist without the world; in Wordsworth's synthetic vision there is little reason to compartmentalize meaning, for the very nature of meaning is that it flows through all. His work often dramatizes the tragedy that arises from fragmented approaches to existence. This is not to say that Wordsworth does not accept the prophecies of Revelation, but the cumulative effect of his works asserts that there is an opportunity to defer, if not halt, the destructive apocalyptic vision of this world, which is, though fallen, not necessarily lost.

One of the most important roles of nature undertaken in this sonnet set and introduced into the series is nature's serving as an intermediary between the body and the soul. Nature translates the language of the soul into the language of the senses, moving body and mind, through the imagination, to a higher consciousness of being, a relatedness to nature linked to God, at times the very palpable perception of God's presence.[5] This concept, not new to the poet's work, is evident in the Snowdon passage in *The Prelude* and in Wordsworth's letter to Dorothy Wordsworth during his 1790 continental tour: "Among the more awful scenes of the Alps . . . my whole soul was turned to Him who produced the terrible majesty before me."[6] The ascent of Snowdon passage, as well as the section that follows Wordsworth's description of that scene as "The perfect image of a mighty Mind . . . that feeds upon infinity" (1805.XIII.69–70), sufficiently demonstrates the role of nature as an intermediary between the language of the senses and the language of the soul:

> One function of such mind had Nature there
> Exhibited by putting forth, and that
> With circumstance most awful and sublime,
> That domination which she oftentimes
> Exerts upon the outward face of things,
> So moulds them, and endues, abstracts, combines,
> Or by abrupt and unhabitual influence
> Doth make one object so impress itself
> Upon all others, and pervade them so
> That even the grossest minds must see and hear
> And cannot chuse but feel. The Power which these
> Acknowledge when thus moved, which Nature thus
> Thrusts forth upon the senses is the express
> Resemblance, in the fulness of its strength
> Made visible, a genuine Counterpart
> And Brother of the glorious faculty
> Which higher minds bear with them as their own.
>   (1805.XIII.74–90)

The poet's attention to the relationship between the body
and the soul, and the associated topic of death, is evidenced
most obviously in the number of references to these terms and
concepts in this sonnet set. Sonnets I.15 to I.25 offer six
references to the word "soul" (sonnets I.16, I.18, I.19, I.20,
and I.23) and one to "spirit," meaning "soul" (sonnet I.20), four
uses of the word "death" (sonnets I.18, I.19, I.20, and I.23),
but six references to the concept of death (for example, "dirges
sung" [sonnet I.19] and "beyond the grave" [sonnet I.24]); two
reference to "Body," (sonnet I.6 and I.20), but twenty-three
references in all to body parts, such as the six in sonnet I.15:
"shoulders curved," "stature tall," "Black hair," "vivid eye,"
"meagre cheek," and nose described as an "eagle's beak."
    It is fitting that sonnet I.20 contains references to soul,
body, and death, for it addresses the effectiveness and appro-
priateness of prayers for the soul of the departed. But other
sonnets in this group pay atypical attention to physical descrip-
tions of the body. Sonnet I.15, which describes Paulinus' appearance, has already been mentioned, but sonnet I.19 on the
Saxon clergy is another example. The priest, whose outward
form is "as bare / As winter trees," has a soul that "is clothed
with fruit divine!" When he is called "forth to breathe the
common air":

> happy are the eyes that meet
> The Apparition; evil thoughts are stayed
> At his approach, and low-bowed necks entreat
> A benediction from his voice or hand;
> Whence grace, through which the heart can understand,
> And vows, that bind the will, in silence made.

In addition to the seventeen references to the body in this
sonnet set, there are also appeals to all five senses, including
three references to breathing and four to voice.[7]
    But the attention given to the body in the context of the
relationship between the body and the soul is only one level
of the poet's concern, for body also refers to the body of Christ
that Christians become part of at baptism. The sonnets in
this group create this larger theological context. Sonnet I.17
addresses baptism and the promise of regenerate life; sonnets

I. 15 and I. 23 focus on the saints Paulinus and Bede, reminding the reader that baptism is a call to sainthood; and sonnet I. 24 offers a congregation of people as the body of Christ building a new church.

People working as the body of Christ is evident, not only in the building of a church, but in the missionary efforts of Augustine in sonnet I. 14, Paulinus in sonnets I. 15 and I. 16, and others in sonnet I. 25; in the work of the clergy and cloistered in sonnets I. 19 to I. 21; in the work of scholars such as Bede in sonnet I. 23; and in the work of Wordsworth himself, who, although he writes as one wanting to escape to a hermitage in sonnet I. 22, does so only as a foil to praise the indefatigable Bede, who died dictating the last words of his translation of the Gospel of St. John.[8] The meaning that arises from the juxtaposition of the two meanings of body, one articulated, the other implied by context, exemplifies the Wordsworthian approach to a synthetic Christian vision.

The Poet in Historical and Religious Contexts

Sonnet I. 22, the first in the series to focus on the poet, is placed in the company of sonnets I. 1 to I. 6 and I. 23, concerning three monks who become saints, Augustine of Canterbury and Paulinus of York, missionaries and archbishops, and Bede, the most profound scholar of his age.

Despite the association by proximity with these great historical and religious figures, the poet more directly identifies himself with the weary chieftain in sonnet I. 21 who retires from the world to become a monk.[9] In the next sonnet the poet writes, "Methinks that to some vacant hermitage / *My* feet would rather turn." Although the chieftain physically withdraws from society, there is a sense that his prayers ("at his side / A bead-roll") serve him and humanity better than did his sword:

> Round the decaying trunk of human pride,
> At morn, and eve, and midnight's silent hour,
> Do penitential cogitations cling;
> Like ivy, round some ancient elm, they twine

In grisly folds and strictures serpentine;
Yet, while they strangle, a fair growth they bring,
For recompense—their own perennial bower.

(I.21)

The imagery of the parasitic vines suggests the consciousness of death and decay, but in this use of his decreasing
time, he gains eternity, represented by the "fair growth," a
"perennial bower." This idea is reminiscent of the "Abundant
recompense" in "Tintern Abbey" (88) and "the faith that looks
through death, / In years that bring the philosophic mind" in
the "Intimations" ode (185–86).

While it is understandable that the poet would allot a significant portion of this set to Paulinus' conversion of King
Edwin and Northumbria, the first major successful conversion
outside of Augustine's conversion of Kent, it is odd (despite
this group's attention to the body and soul) that one of the
three sonnets given over to the story of the conversion focuses
almost solely on Paulinus' physical appearance. Of the twenty-
three references to the body or body parts, six (more than one-
quarter) appear in sonnet I.15, "Paulinus." Perhaps the poet
is drawn to his own likeness. With even limited familiarity
with portraits of the younger Wordsworth, the similarity is
recognizable:

Mark him, of shoulders curved, and stature tall,
Black hair, and vivid eye, and meagre cheek,
His prominent feature like an eagle's beak;
A Man whose aspect doth at once appal
And strike with reverence.

Bede's description of Paulinus may have struck Wordsworth, as much as anyone is intrigued by the possibility of a
Doppelgänger. This idea is reinforced by Paulinus' and Wordsworth's similar teaching missions. The purpose of the *Ecclesiastical Sonnets* as a means of coming to terms with a historically
based Christian identity is new to the oeuvre with this work.
But the teaching mission, the poet's fulfilling of his ministry,
is clearly set forth in the conclusion of the 1805 *Prelude:*

Oh! yet a few short years of useful life,
And all will be complete, thy race be run,
Thy monument of glory will be raised.
Then, though, too weak to tread the ways of truth,
This Age fall back to old idolatry,
Though men return to servitude as fast
As the tide ebbs, to ignominy and shame
By Nations sink together, we shall still
Find solace in the knowledge which we have,
Bless'd with true happiness if we may be
United helpers forward of a day
Of firmer trust, joint-labourers in a work
(Should Providence such grace to us vouchsafe)
Of their redemption, surely yet to come.
Prophets of Nature, we to them will speak
A lasting inspiration, sanctified
By reason and by truth; what we have loved,
Others will love; and we may teach them how;
Instruct them how the mind of man becomes
A thousand times more beautiful than the earth
On which he dwells, above this Frame of things
(Which, 'mid all revolutions in the hopes
And fears of men, doth still remain unchanged)
In beauty exalted, as it is itself
Of substance and of fabric more divine.

(XIII.428–52)

The opening of this passage with "thy race be run" resonates
with the message of Paul's letter to Timothy: "watch thou in
all things, endure afflictions, do the work of an evangelist,
make full proof of thy ministry. For I am now ready to be
offered, and the time of my departure is at hand. I have fought
a good fight, I have finished my course, I have kept the faith"
(2 Timothy 4:5–7).

Like John, the poet of the *Ecclesiastical Sonnets* baptizes
the reader in the Holy River of his poetic creation, which
merges poetry, religion, nature, and all human experience
throughout time. There is, in addition, a coalescence through
identification of the reader with the poet because of the peculiar personal nature of the presentation. The Holy River is the
central symbol of the sonnet series, the history of the Church,

the creation of the poet, yet also the call to baptism, salvation, and ministry. There can be no doubt that the *Ecclesiastical Sonnets* are a part of Wordsworth's attempt to fulfull his ministry.

Although sonnet I.22, on the poet's ostensible longing for withdrawal from the world, serves as a response to sonnet I.21 on the chieftain turned monk, sonnet I.22 also serves as a foil to sonnet I.23, "Reproof," which praises Bede's active life dedicated to perpetual service:

> But what if One, through grove or flowery mead,
> Indulging thus at will the creeping feet
> Of a voluptuous indolence, should meet
> Thy hovering Shade, O venerable Bede!
> The saint, the scholar, from a circle freed
> Of toil stupendous, in a hallowed seat
> Of learning, where thou heard'st the billows beat
> On a wild coast, rough monitors to feed
> Perpetual industry. Sublime Recluse!
> The recreant soul, that dares to shun the debt
> Imposed on human kind, must first forget
> Thy diligence, thy unrelaxing use
> Of a long life; and in the hour of death,
> The last dear service of thy passing breath!

Bede died at the age of sixty-two, dictating with his last breath a translation of St. John's Gospel. The energy of the content and meter in lines 5 through 14, after the lethargic beginning, reflects the poet's imitation of Bede's indefatigable labors. The poet's identification with Bede is suggested by the content, style, and context of this sonnet and in the fact that both scholars invested extensive research in the writing of Church histories. The parallel between Wordsworth and Bede draws attention to the interfacing of poetry, history, and faith.

As a group, sonnets I.21 to I.23, aside from their distinctive poetic beauty, exhibit some of the significant features of the series: the interpenetration of nature and the Church; the resonances from the poet's other work; the interrelating of the sonnets, which achieves coherence among 132 parts, which is no mean feat; and the evidence of the personal role of the poet in the design and purpose of the work. This latter point becomes clearer as the work progresses. Sonnet set I.15 to I.25 markedly demonstrates that the series is not merely an objective endeavor to record the Church's past, but a personal, spiritual, and intellectual journey designed to assimilate the communal Christian past into the poet's individual Christian identity.

Fancy and the Supernatural

Fancy is introduced into the series in sonnet I.18, "Apology," which argues that even imperfect faith has value.[10] Fancy's introduction begins a series of appearances throughout this sonnet set of good and evil spirits, visions, and ghosts. Sonnet I.18, beautiful and intense, is important in refuting some of the common, superficially informed arguments about Wordsworth's encroaching orthodoxy—arguments that often portray his attachment to his faith as a state of psychic rigor mortis.

The sonnet argues that because "Death, darkness, danger, are our natural lot" and because we see as through a glass darkly, for all that the wisest can know, "evil Spirits *may* our walk attend." It makes sense, therefore, to allow flexibility in one's imaginings for "*good* Spirits . . . to breathe a note / Of elevation."[11] Sonnet I.18 concludes:

> Nor doubt that golden cords
> Of good works, mingling with the visions, raise
> The Soul to purer worlds: and *who* the line
> Shall draw, the limits of the power define,
> That even imperfect faith to man affords.

This is a liberal, practical, and certainly not stiffly orthodox approach,[12] whose argument cleverly turns doubt against itself. This sonnet is powerful testimony to the poet's sane and balanced view of the role of fancy in faith and religion. It asks, who are we to scorn conceptions that help people to live better lives? The benefits of even imperfect faith, defended in this sonnet, are paired in sonnet I.24 with good works, which even

when done for the wrong reasons (hope of reward or fear of
punishment) benefit the individual and society.

The notion of visions that "raise / The Soul to purer worlds"
is seen again in sonnet I.22, in which the poet describes a
sylvan retreat where

> under sylvan arches cool,
> Fit haunt of shapes whose glorious equipage
> Would elevate my dreams.

Fancy's assistance in raising the soul's consciousness appears
also in sonnets I.19, I.20, and I.23. In sonnet I.19, the priest

> when service worthy of his care
> Has called him forth to breathe the common air,
> Might seem a saintly Image from its shrine
> Descended.

He is described as an "Apparition" who inspires happiness and
stays evil thoughts. And through this fanciful vision aided by
grace, "A benediction from his voice or hand" moves people
to make vows that bind the will.

In sonnet I.20, "Confession ministers the pang to soothe /
In him who at the ghost of guilt doth start." The final example
in sonnet I.23 touches the poet personally and merges the
doctrinal examples with the poetic work. First, sonnet I.22
describes the poet's ostensible longing for "some vacant hermitage . . . near a brook" where he could experience the world
displaced even further by viewing it in the reflections of a
"translucent pool." The conclusion relinquishes even bird
song:

> nor should e'er the crested fowl
> From thorp or vill his matins sound for me,
> Tired of the world and all its industry.

But then, out of this indolence rises sonnet I.23 with "But
what if One . . . should meet / Thy hovering Shade, O venera-
ble Bede!" The rhythm surges with the rousing content and
the sonnet verifies the ability of a vision—and poetry—to
heighten the soul, if not to inspire and motivate service.

With the close of this sonnet set, the role of the Church in Wordsworth's synthetic vision becomes clear. The Church serves as a unifier, a source of stability, and a peacemaker. In sonnets I.14 to I.17, the Word conquers without the sword—with "bare words," a "silver Cross . . . instead / Of [a] martial banner" (I.14). The transience of life portrayed in sonnet I.16, "Persuasion," with the sparrow representing the soul's visitation in the body, and even the wholesale slaughter of the monks at the monastery of Bangor in sonnet I.12 is juxtaposed with the timelessness and stability of the Church. As a context for baptism, the Church unifies Christians in their call to service and sainthood in the body of Christ. The Church functions as a unifying element, interrelating human experience and psychic life, combating alienation in a fallen world, and encouraging harmony and a sense of belonging in humanity and between humanity and the natural world. The Church is, at its best, a cultural, societal, public assertion of humanity's belief in its capacity for right action and its susceptibility to divine inspiration and guidance. It offers a context for the recognition of what is best about humanity despite an awareness of its limitations and weaknesses.

At its best, the Church nurtures humaneness, compassion, selflessness, duty, and commitment to a higher value system. But because the Church is a human endeavor in the fallen world, even though divinely inspired, the Church is liable to suffer from shortsightedness and failures. Wordsworth is far from blind to these shortcomings, as a substantial part of the series attests; but overall, the concept of the Church plays a fundamental role in Wordsworth's synthetic worldview. The poet remarks to Bishop Wordsworth: "Almost all [the Church's] errors are corruptions of what is good."[13]

In addition, sonnets I.15 to I.25 impressively demonstrate the primacy of nature in Wordsworth's perception of the Church and its history. The series resonates with the dynamic interplay between the ecclesiastical narrative and the narrative's prolific imagery of the natural world. This dynamic interplay is not conflictive but synthetic, characteristic of the poet's expansive unifying vision.

The impress of the imagery nurtures a confluence of nature

and the Church. In the process, the mind of humanity is linked
to the Church through nature. This process is facilitated by
the wedding of the mind to nature in Wordsworth's previous
works; however, this union is not treated as being complete,
nor is it taken for granted; instead, it is reinforced within
the *Ecclesiastical Sonnets* and becomes part of the creative,
organic process that continues to evolve into a comprehensible
synthesis of the spiritual, emotional, intellectual, and physical
worlds. The poet's cross-referencing of his works through direct reference, allusion, and subtle resonances reflects his
stance on the value of perceiving experience in context—in
the context of one's own experience and that of others, in the
context of one's own time and of the past, and even in the
context of experience projected into the future. "Higher
minds," Wordsworth says,

> hold fit converse with the spiritual world,
> And with the generations of mankind
> Spread over time, past, present, and to come,
> Age after age, till Time shall be no more.
> (*Prelude*, 1850.XIV.90, 108–11)

6

Faith and Governance:
A Fissure Between Nature and the
Church in Sonnets I.26 to I.39

The narrative of this final set of Part I moves swiftly, covering about 350 years from the reign of Alfred into the reign of King John (1199–1216). It has a three-part structure: Sonnets I.26 to I.30 dramatize both positive and negative aspects of the relationship of church and state, with the beneficial influences of Alfred, his descendants, and Canute, contrasting with the destructiveness of Dunstan; sonnets I.31 to I.35 focus on the Norman Conquest and the Crusades, whose warrior leaders were often motivated as much, if not more, by political zeal and greed as by religious fervor; and sonnets I.36 to I.39 vehemently attack the abuse of papal power that interferes with the beneficial governance of the state and the well-being of society.

The narrative of this set is also distinguished by a significant increase in the role of historical figures. While the first twenty-five sonnets in Part I refer to about twenty, with only six sonnets focusing on famous figures (Gregory in sonnet I.13, Augustine in sonnet I.14, Paulinus in sonnet I.15, Bede in sonnet I.23, and Wordsworth himself in sonnets I.1 and I.22), ten sonnets in this last set of fourteen focus on famous historical figures (Alfred, Dunstan, Edgar, Canute, Edward the Confessor, Hereward, Pope Urban II, Richard I, Pope Innocent III, King Henry II, King John, Emperor Frederick I [Barbarossa], and Pope Alexander III).

The emphasis on historical figures is a function of this set's criticism of the Roman Church. The criticism spans six sonnets that vehemently attack the abuse of papal power. It is important to note that the poet's criticism of the Roman Church focuses on men who have lost sight of their Christian missions and who use their positions of power to worship at the altar of their own egos. It is also important to note that the poet balances this criticism with a delineation in Part II of the benefits of the Roman Church. This censure and praise reveals the poet's balanced approach to the Roman Church and contradicts the often unquestioned acceptance of critics' assertions about the poet's narrow-minded religious orthodoxy.

The series' central theme of the interpenetration of nature and the Church takes on an interesting modulation in the conclusion to Part I. When influential Church figures give themselves over to foolish political power plays, nature realigns itself with the Word and the concept of Christianity against the misguided representatives of the institution. This shift occurs in the criticism of Dunstan, blamed for the renewed Danish invasions, in sonnet I.29; of Pope Innocent III, for the 1208 interdict, in sonnet I.36; of the monks, for the scourging of Henry II at Becket's shrine and for Pandolphus' debasing of King John, in sonnet I.37; of Pope Alexander, for the humiliation of Emperor Frederick I, in sonnet I.38; and of papal abuse of power in general, in sonnet I.39. This fissure between nature and the Roman Church worsens, so that by the conclusion of this set only nature seems free of papal dominion:

> Unless to Peter's Chair the viewless wind
> Must come and ask permission when to blow,
> What further empire would it have?
>
> (I.39)

Although the topics of war, destruction, betrayal, and death weigh heavily on the narrative of this set, three sonnets (sonnet I.26, "Alfred"; sonnet I.27, "His descendants"; and sonnet I.30, "Canute") highlight the human potential for good; the last, in particular, shimmers with a warm, diffuse light of hope for the beneficial interaction of faith and governance. As a function of this optimism, these three sonnets distinguish themselves with their profusion of nature and music imagery, with twenty-one nature images and seven references to music, while the remaining eleven sonnets in this set average only three nature images and fewer than one reference to music per sonnet. These three sonnets exemplify the theme of the interpenetration of nature and the Church by emphasizing the benefits to society of a government inspired by a faith linked to the earth through nature. They are the only positive sonnets in this last group of fourteen.

Sonnets I.26, I.27, and I.30 will be discussed first, focusing on the beneficial interfacing of church and state, piety and governance—an interaction highlighted and praised by a profusion of music and nature imagery. The second part of this chapter discusses the six sonnets (I.28, I.29, and I.36 to I.39) that portray the relationship gone awry between the church and state and the subsequent realignment of nature and music imagery with Christianity and the Word against the Church as a political tool of papal dominion. The third part of this chapter addresses the central group of sonnets (I.31 to I.35) that serves as a transition into the tempestuous attack on papal abuse.

Sonnets I.26, I.27, and I.30: Alfred and Canute

In sonnet I.26, the piety of the great ruler Alfred inspires Wordsworth's praise:

> Behold a pupil of the monkish gown,
> The pious ALFRED, King to Justice dear!
> Lord of the harp and liberating spear;
> Mirror of Princes!

Like the saintly and indefatigable Bede, "Ease from this noble miser of his time / No moment steals"; Alfred overcomes the maladies that plagued him his whole life ("pain narrows not his cares") with strength fortified by faith. His achievements

are set forth in this sonnet in an expansive analogy to nature,
marked by continued references to his piety:

> Indigent Renown
> Might range the starry ether for a crown
> Equal to *his* deserts, who, like the year,
> Pours forth his bounty, like the day doth cheer,
> And awes like night with mercy-tempered frown
> . . . .
> Though small his kingdom as a spark or gem,
> Of Alfred boasts remote Jerusalem,
> And Christian India, through her wide-spread clime,
> In sacred converse gifts with Alfred shares.

Nature imagery is intensified in sonnet I.27, "His descendants," in which Alfred's family is compared to a strong and
spreading oak that survives fierce storms.[1] The sonnet opens
with water imagery:

> a bitter shower
> Fell on thy tomb; but emulative power
> Flowed in thy line through undegenerate veins.

Water imagery continues with two references to tempests, but
the dominant image is of a massive oak that nurtures flowers
in its shade:

> The Race of Alfred covet glorious pains
> When dangers threaten, dangers ever new!
> Black tempests bursting, blacker still in view!
> But manly sovereignty its hold retains;
> The root sincere, the branches bold to strive
> With the fierce tempest, while, within the round
> Of their protection, gentle virtues thrive;
> As oft, 'mid some green plot of open ground,
> Wide as the oak extends its dewy gloom,
> The fostered hyacinths spread their purple bloom.

Sonnet I.30 exhibits the synthetic process of the poet's vision: poetry ("Royal Minstrel," "accordant Rhyme," and "Piety
and Song") joins forces with nature, faith, and music to succor

the "suffering Earth." Reminiscent of the earlier sonnets in
Part I, this sonnet emphasizes water imagery, with Canute
and his retinue rowing past the "Monks in Ely chanting service
high." The sonnet picks up and enhances the music imagery
begun in sonnet I.26 with "Lord of the harp," highlights the
important role of piety, and melds all three (water, music, and
poetry) with the piety that began this group ("pious Alfred,
King to Justice dear!" in sonnet I.26). Sonnet I.30 appears
below with emphasis added to highlight the interweaving of
nature with piety, and of water imagery with poetry/song:

> A pleasant *music floats* along the *Mere*,
> From Monks in Ely *chanting* service high,
> While-as Canùte the King is *rowing* by:
> "My *Oarsmen*," quoth the mighty King, "draw near,
> That we the sweet *song* of the Monks may hear!"
> He listens (all past conquests and all schemes
> Of future vanishing like empty dreams)
> Heart-touched, and haply not without a *tear*.
> The royal *Minstrel*, ere the *choir* is still,
> While his free Barge skims the smooth *flood* along,
> Gives to that rapture an accordant *Rhyme*.
> O suffering Earth! be thankful; sternest clime
> And rudest age are subject to the thrill
> Of heaven-descended *Piety* and *Song*.

Sonnets I.28, I.29, and I.36 to I.39: Papal Abuse of Power

The previous group of sonnets (I.26, I.27, and I.30), strong
in nature and music imagery, demonstrate an interpenetration
of nature and the Church manifested in an ideal interfacing of
faith and governance. Six of the remaining sonnets in this final
section of Part I, however, reveal the dark side of the Church's
participation in the fallen world: pride and papal abuse of
power. The susceptibility of the Church to err is quite in
character with Wordsworth's overall treatment of the Church
as divinely inspired, but as a human institution, subject to all
the weaknesses of human endeavor.

The Church's fallen nature is not an excuse, however. The
vehemence of the poet's attack on the abuse of papal power

shows that, despite his sane and balanced approach to the
human condition, he does not take kindly to human folly
couched in the self-important guise of institutional decree.
The series' central theme of the interpenetration of nature and
the Church modulates when the Church is sullied by pride:
nature imagery realigns with Christian faith and the Word
against the misguided representatives of the institution.

The six sonnets that vehemently attack the misuse of papal
power are sonnet I.28, "Influence abused"; sonnet I.29, "Danish conquests"; sonnet I.36, "An interdict"; sonnet I.37, "Papal
abuses"; sonnet I.38, "Scene in Venice"; and sonnet I.39,
"Papal dominion." These include the four final sonnets of Part
I, closing the first third of the series on a markedly negative,
bitter, and angry note. The negativity of these six sonnets is
reflected in the meager music and nature imagery. There is
only one reference to music and that is to its absence: in sonnet
I.36, during the 1208 interdict, the church "bells are dumb."
One water image appears in sonnet I.29 with "northern main"
in reference to the Danish invasions. In sonnet I.37 the word
"Stream" refers to the historical "voyage we pursue," and an
"angry Ocean roar[ing] a vain appeal" refers most directly to
the response to the insulting abuse of papal power in the
scourging of Henry II and the debasing of King John. The
remaining nature imagery is straightforward aligned with the
Word and the human condition against the abuse associated
with the institution.

The imagery that then becomes associated with the Church
moves into the unnatural, into the supernatural. For instance,
sonnet I.28 describes Dunstan:

        Behold, pre-signified,
    The Might of spiritual sway! his thoughts, his dreams,
    Do in the supernatural world abide:
    So vaunt a throng of Followers, filled with pride
    In what they see of virtues pushed to extremes,
    And sorceries of talent misapplied.

In sonnet I.36, in response to the interdict,

> Fancies thickly come
> Into the pensive heart ill fortified,
> And comfortless despairs the soul benumb.

And sonnet I.38 refers to "Black Demons hovering o'er [the pope's] mitred head." The group concludes with the pope's "magic wand" in sonnet I.39.

The poet's separation of the Word from the institution can be seen in sonnet I.29, which begins, "Woe to the Crown that doth the Cowl obey!" The sonnet refers to Dunstan's influence on Edgar, which seems to have precipitated renewed Danish invasions, ironically helping to restore and spread pagan religion:

> But Gospel-truth is potent to allay
> Fierceness and rage; and soon the cruel Dane
> Feels, through the influence of her gentle reign,
> His native superstitions melt away.
> Thus, often, when thick gloom the east o'ershrouds,
> The full-orbed Moon, slow-climbing, doth appear
> Silently to consume the heavy clouds;
> *How* no one can resolve; but every eye
> Around her sees, while air is hushed, a clear
> And widening circuit of ethereal sky.

The silent, gentle rising and muted light of the moon in the "ethereal sky" reflects the mysterious and "gentle" conquest of the Word ("Gospel-truth") over the "thick gloom" and "heavy clouds" of the invaders' fierceness, rage, and cruelty.

In the final four sonnets, nature suffers along with humanity under the papal oppression and shares in the general outrage. In sonnet I.36, the interdict, set upon England to punish King John for refusing to accept the pope's recommendation of Stephen Langton as Archbishop of Canterbury, closed the churches and forbade religious rites that provide comfort, guidance, and stability to the individual and to human relations:

> Straight from the sun and tainted air's embrace
> All sacred things are covered: cheerful morn
> Grows sad as night—no seemly garb is worn,

> Nor is a face allowed to meet a face
> With natural smiles of greeting. Bells are dumb;
> Ditches are graves—funeral rites denied;
> And in the churchyard he must take his bride
> Who dares be wedded! Fancies thickly come
> Into the pensive heart ill fortified,
> And comfortless despairs the soul benumb.

As nature shared the oppression of the Christians in the earlier sonnets, the first three lines of this sonnet illustrate that nature shares and suffers the interdict along with humanity.

Sonnet I.37, already mentioned for its two examples of water imagery, aligns "Stream" with "the voyage we pursue," and "angry Ocean" with the response to the papal abuse of Henry II and King John. The scourging of Henry and the debasing of John ordered by the papacy are, according to this sonnet, examples of bizarre, unnatural actualities that challenge the capacity of the imagination in terms of what it may expect from reality:

> The gross materials of this world present
> A marvellous study of wild accident;
> Uncouth proximities of old and new;
> And bold transfigurations, more untrue
> (As might be deemed) to disciplined intent
> Than aught the sky's fantastic element,
> When most fantastic, offers to the view.

The bizarre oppression continues in sonnet I.38, which refers to the legendary degradation of Emperor Frederick I by Pope Alexander III. Here the "common dignity of man" is aligned with "earth" and "outraged Nature":

> Black Demons hovering o'er his mitred head,
> To Caesar's Successor the Pontiff spake;
> "Ere I absolve thee, stoop! that on thy neck
> Levelled with earth this foot of mine may tread."
> Then he, who to the altar had been led,
> He, whose strong arm the Orient could not check,
> He, who had held the Soldan at his beck,
> Stooped, of all glory disinherited,

And even the common dignity of man!—
Amazement strikes the crowd: while many turn
Their eyes away in sorrow, others burn
With scorn, invoking a vindictive ban
From outraged Nature; but the sense of most
In abject sympathy with power is lost.

In sonnet I.39, papal abuse reaches the apex of its voracity.
Only the wind seems free of papal dominion. All nature reacts
to the papal onslaught:

Unless to Peter's Chair the viewless wind
Must come and ask permission when to blow,
What further empire would it have? for now
A ghostly Domination, unconfined
As that by dreaming Bards to Love assigned,
Sits there in sober truth—to raise the low,
Perplex the wise, the strong to overthrow;
Through earth and heaven to bind and to unbind!—
Resist—the thunder quails thee!—crouch—rebuff
Shall be thy recompense! from land to land
The ancient thrones of Christendom are stuff
For occupation of a magic wand,
And 'tis the Pope that wields it:—whether rough
Or smooth his front, our world is in his hand!

Sonnets I.31 to I.35: Fractures in the Vision

Sonnets I.31 to I.35, which address the Norman Conquest
and the Crusades, serve as a transition into the modulation of
the nature/Church relationship. The character of the modulation, however, allows for the vehement attack on the papacy
without weakening the bond between nature and faith.
Through these sonnets, a fissure emerges between three aspects that until now have been interfaced in Part I: nature,
the human drama, and the Church. The interweaving of these
aspects, which has been a generative, organic force throughout, begins to unravel.

In sonnet I.31, for instance, the human drama is oddly
alienated from nature and the Church. As William the Con-

queror decrees blackouts to squelch political resistance by
forbidding night meetings,

> stars shine;
> But . . . the lights that cherish household cares
> And festive gladness

are extinguished. Allowed to burn, however, are the "tapers
of the sacred choirs." The conquest,

> studious to expel
> Old laws, and ancient customs to derange,
> To Creed or Ritual brings no fatal change.

Nature and the Church remain aligned but are strangely ex-
empt from humanity, which suffers oppression by the "force
that daunts, and cunning that ensnares!"

But the peculiar stance of nature in this sonnet in relation
to the human drama is a fragmentary perception, a function of
the swift, ubiquitous, shocking cruelty of the harrying of the
English countryside. The stance reflects the confused moment
when humanity suddenly feels alienated from its surroundings;
however, this stance is not indicative of an actual disjunction
between nature and humanity. As the next sonnet testifies,
nature is not uninvolved in the human drama.

Sonnet I.32 refers to the Normans' bloody advance through
the English countryside in which adults, children, and farm
animals are mutilated and slaughtered and homes and fields
are "laid waste." The Normans' attachment to the Church
had no effect at this time upon their discernment of humane
behavior, although the Church seems responsible eventually
for some societal advances. Trevelyan explains:

> The Normans were quite as inhumane as the Anglo-Saxons or
> Danes of contemporary England, and being more active and
> industrious they committed many more deeds of revolting cru-
> elty. The lopping off of hands and the gouging out of eyes of
> prisoners and rebels, wholesale massacre of populations, and
> deliberate devastation of whole districts, were among the Nor-
> man methods of warfare, as England was soon to learn to her

cost. The Norman, devoted servant of the Church as he had now become, had advanced little if at all beyond the heathen Viking in point of humane conduct. But in knowledge and organizing power he had advanced. The Church taught barbarians to organize society, and it was this better organization of society, even more than the precept and example of the Church herself, that eventually taught men to take the first halting steps in the direction of humanity and justice.[2]

This sonnet reveals a particularly important aspect of the series' interpenetration of nature and the Church: as nature suffers and is stripped away (fields are burned and animals are slaughtered), humanity looks directly through its faith to God. The Church is neither present nor instrumental. It is as if without nature, the Church is without context:

> The Saxons, overpowered
> By wrong triumphant through its own excess,
> From fields laid waste, from house and home devoured
> By flames, look up to heaven and crave redress
> From God's eternal justice. Pitiless
> Though men be, there are angels that can feel
> For wounds that death alone has power to heal,
> For penitent guilt, and innocent distress.
>
> (I.32)

The drama evolves without the Church, but with faith and ritual, for the people "canonize" Hereward, the rebel who valiantly fought against the Normans, "in their hearts" and value the "sacred earth where his dear relics lie." The stripping process in this sonnet manifests a direct movement through nature to God. The Church, if it is present here, is present only at a remove, in the concept of the ritual of canonization, for the canonization of Hereward actually occurs in people's hearts without the aid of the institution's paraphernalia. And although much of nature is stripped away—"fields laid waste"—nature persists at the end of the sonnet:

> And far above the mine's most precious ore
> the least small pittance of bare mould they prize
> Scooped from the sacred earth where his dear relics lie.

Sonnets I.33 to I.35 begin with "The Council of Clermont," called in 1095 by Pope Urban II to proclaim the first crusade. They then move to the crusades themselves, which "Upheave, so it seems, from her natural station / All Christendom." They conclude with a sonnet on Richard I, noted for his exploits in the third crusade in regaining the lands that had been won in the first crusade but subsequently taken by Saladin. The sonnets reflect a manifestation of the worst possible interfusion of church and state, religion and nationalism: In sonnet I.33, in response to the pontiff's proclamation of the first crusade,

> "God willeth it," from hill to hill rebounds,
> And, in awe-stricken Countries far and nigh,
> Through "Nature's hollow arch" that voice resounds.

In sonnet I.34,

>   they sweep along (was never
> So huge a host!)—to tear from the Unbeliever
> The precious Tomb, their haven of salvation.[3]

In sonnet I.35:

> My Song, a fearless homager, would attend
> Thy thundering battle-axe as it cleaves the press
> Of war, but duty summons her away
> To tell—how, finding in the rash distress
> Of those Enthusiasts a subservient friend,
> To giddier heights hath clomb the Papal sway.

While nature imagery occurs in sonnets I.33 to I.35, the instances are few, passive, and often literal. Water imagery, so symbolically central to the series, here is only very literally "Bosphorus" (I.34) and "sailing o'er the midland brine" (I.35), and figuratively "the current of their arms" and "they sweep along" (I.34). As for nature imagery, in sonnet I.34, the "Grecian hills" will not long detain the "thickening swarms" of invaders, and in sonnet I.35 there is an animal reference to Richard, "of courage leonine."

Sonnet I.33 offers an agricultural image of sowing: "War-

riors, go, / With prayers and blessings we your path will sow."
As weak as it is, this is perhaps the strongest example of some
remaining interaction of nature and the Church in this section
in which the relationship weakens. Interestingly, though, sonnet I.33 uses an echo, which recalls the powerful scene in
sonnet I.11 in which "hallelujahs tost from hill to hill—/
[achieved] instant victory" over the invading Saxons and Picts.
In sonnet I.33 the multitude responds to the pontiff's proclamation of the first crusade with " 'God willeth it' [which] from
hill to hill rebounds." Unlike the use in sonnet I.11, however,
nature in sonnet I.33 is passive; it is merely a "hollow arch"
through which the "voice resounds." It is as though nature
suffers a shock-induced paralysis. Sonnet I.11, on the contrary,
offers a rich profusion of imagery that portrays nature's participation in the human drama. The intensity of "O wretched
Land! whose tears have flowed like fountains" highlights by
contrast that the dynamic interplay of nature and the human
drama gradually slips away from the transitional group of sonnets I.31 to I.35.

Sonnets I.26 to I.39, the final set of Part I, covering about
350 years from the reign of Alfred to the reign of King John,
introduces and highlights the role of the Church in the political
history of England. This role, which will be a strong narrative
thread in Part II, is important in forcing a modulation in the
series' central theme of the interpenetration of nature and the
Church. The significant feature of Part I is that as the poet's
vision argues for a synthesis of nature and the Church, nature
and the dignity of common humanity remain the foundational
context. Nature, as a participant in the human drama, more
responsive to human suffering, and subject itself to suffering,
remains consistently closer to God. It is the Church within
this context that has value to the poet, for when the institution
defies nature, which to the poet includes respect for the dignity
of common humanity, the poet realigns the work's imagery
to isolate the foolish and offensive behavior in a frightening
dimension characterized by an absence of music and an unre-
sponsive natural landscape. This dimension may be likened to
the alienating "thingscape" of a Dali painting. The recognized
poetic and philosophical power of the poet of *The Prelude*

resonates in the *Ecclesiastical Sonnets* for those who recognize that he is devoting his attention to a different region of the vast cosmography of his works, epic in scope, but unified by a spiritual, synthetic vision.

7

Part II: The Synthetic Vision

Part II of the series covers about 433 years, from the reign of Henry III (1216–72) to the end of the reign of Charles I (1625–49), and has roughly a three-part narrative structure. Countering the vehement criticism of the Roman Church at the close of Part I, the first ten sonnets of Part II delineate significant benefits of the Roman Church. This group ends with "Enough!" and there follows a series of ten sonnets that renews the attack on the Roman Church for its corruption, abuse of monastic power, and oppression and persecution of Protestant thinkers, from Peter Waldo to Wycliffe. Five sonnets follow that address the dissolution of the monasteries and offer certain regrets at the loss of the saints and the Virgin Mary. The remaining sonnets trace the undulation of power between church and state, between Catholics and Protestants, and between the instituting of reforms and the undoing of reforms.[1] This chaotic but rich ferment ultimately gives rise to the uniqueness of the Anglican Church, whose stable but dynamic presence graces the Church as an institution, the Anglican Communion, and the British nation. The grace of this presence and its service to the individual and society are reflected in Part III.

Nature continues in Part II to function as a participatory context for the human drama (especially sonnets II.1, II.3, II.7, and II.8), here viewed from the perspective of the history

of the Church. The modulation of the theme of the interpenetration of nature and the Church, in which nature realigns
itself with faith and the Word against the Church during its
abuse of papal power (particularly the concluding four sonnets
of Part I) is carried forward into Part II and dominates the
second group of ten sonnets, which criticizes the Roman
Church for its persecution of reformers, abuse of power, and
corruption (II.2, II.11 to II.14, II.17, and II.32).

But what distinguishes Part II is its intensification of the
theme of the interpenetration of nature and the Church to the
point of boldly setting forth a synthetic vision in which the
boundaries of traditionally distinct conceptual categories (humanity, nature, Church, and God) interfuse. The dynamic
interfacing of nature and the Church progresses to a stage of
merged metaphorical identity in which the Church is endowed
with attributes of nature (sonnets II.2, II.10, and II.28). With
the concluding sonnets of Part II, the synthetic process advances to include, not merged identities, but bonding by analogy, of nature and God in sonnet II.46 and of nature and
religion in a set of two sonnets, II.43 and II.44.

A key sonnet in Part II that begins to show the emphasis on
this synthesis is sonnet II.21, "Dissolution of the monasteries."
The sixteenth-century dissolution of the monasteries because
of their corruption leaves wounds on the psychological and
literal landscapes. But nature heals both kinds of wounds by
converting the ruins into a leafy sanctuary for animals and into
a symbol of the active beneficent presence of nature in the
often faulty human drama:

> Threats come which no submission may assuage,
> No sacrifices avert, no power dispute;
> The tapers shall be quenched, the belfries mute,
> And, 'mid their choirs unroofed by selfish rage,
> The warbling wren shall find a leafy cage;
> The gadding bramble hang her purple fruit;
> And the green lizard and the gilded newt
> Lead unmolested lives, and die of age.
> The owl of evening and the woodland fox
> For their abode the shrines of Waltham choose:
> Proud Glastonbury can no more refuse

To stoop her head before these desperate shocks—
She whose high pomp displaced, as story tells,
Arimathean Joseph's wattled cells.

The active beneficent presence of nature reminds the reader
of the symbolic impress of the scenes in, for instance, "Tintern
Abbey" and "Hart-Leap Well." The interaction of nature and
the Church in this sonnet offers consoling psychological and
spiritual closure to the vehement criticism of the Roman
Church begun in Part I and continued in the second group of
sonnets of Part II (sonnets II.11 to II.20).

This tendency toward healing, which blends the boundaries
of categories in an evolution toward synthesis, is evidenced in
the untitled introductory sonnets to Part II (sonnets II.1 and
II.2), which follow the lacerating attack that concludes Part I.
The calm and thoughtful stance of these introductory sonnets
views the papal perversion of power as a sample of the behavior
that led to the Fall, for the Church as a human institution is
subject to err. Overcoming the bitter indignation that closes
Part I, and seeing "Man" and the "Church" as actors subject
to the fallible script of the drama of the fallen world, sonnet
II.1 argues for "Charity" in even the "sternest sentence," and
prepares for the introduction in sonnet II.2 of a sonnet set that
delineates significant benefits of the Roman Church:

How soon—alas! did Man, created pure—
By Angels guarded, deviate from the line
Prescribed to duty:—woeful forfeiture
He made by wilful breach of law divine.
With like perverseness did the Church abjure
Obedience to her Lord, and haste to twine,
'Mid Heaven-born flowers that shall for aye endure,
Weeds on whose front the world has fixed her sign.
O Man,—if with thy trials thus it fares,
If good can smooth the way to evil choice,
From all rash censure be the mind kept free;
He only judges right who weighs, compares,
And, in the sternest sentence which his voice
Pronounces, ne'er abandons Charity.

(II.1)

And,

> From false assumption rose, and fondly hailed
> By superstition, spread the Papal power;
> Yet do not deem the Autocracy prevailed
> Thus only, even in error's darkest hour.
> She daunts, forth-thundering from her spiritual tower,
> Brute rapine, or with gentle lure she tames.
> Justice and Peace through Her uphold their claims;
> And Chastity finds many a sheltering bower.
> Realm there is none that if controuled or swayed
> By her commands partakes not, in degree,
> Of good, o'er manners, arts and arms, diffused:
> Yes, to thy domination, Roman See,
> Though miserably, oft monstrously, abused
> By blind ambition, be this tribute paid.
>
>   (II.2)

But following the group of sonnets on the benefits of the Roman Church rises yet another attack (sonnets II.11 to II.20), opening the wounds that were ostensibly healed by the introductory sonnets. Hence the necessity for sonnet II.21, which heals the wounds significantly, not with rhetoric—even sincere rhetoric—but meaningfully with the unqualified forgiveness of nature.

The two-phase resolution reflects the unfortunately characteristic disparity between human longing for transcendant good and inadequate capacities for achieving it. The sincere desire for graciousness in sonnet II.1 materializes in praise of the Roman Church in sonnet II.2, but it is not sustained, for the sonnet closes with a wary, wounded, reluctant attitude:

> Yes, to thy dominion, Roman See,
> Though miserably, oft monstrously, abused
> By blind ambition, be this tribute paid.

The ambivalence is temporarily overcome, and ten sonnets follow on the benefits of the Roman Church. But then the difficulty of attaining unqualified forgiveness with true charity surfaces in a ten-sonnet renewed attack. The conflict of mind is not successfully resolved until intellectual concepts are merged with nature in sonnet II.21.

Indeed, the genuineness of the desire for forgiveness and charity is evidenced in the subcontext created in sonnet II.1 by the proximity of "Man," "Church," and nature (in the form of "flowers" and "Weeds"). Nature offers a divinely inspired context of reconciliation, a home for the manifestation of "Heaven-born flowers," and also a patient, accepting base for the "Weeds" that symbolize the fallen world.[2]

By giving human sinfulness a correlative in nature, Wordsworth reinforces the concept of nature's participation in the human drama, dynamically interweaving nature and humanity. With the Church as a manifestation of human endeavor, then nature, humanity, and the Church coalesce in an interaction reinforced throughout Part II.

This interplay of concepts is achieved partly by endowing the Church with characteristics of nature. For instance, in sonnet II.2, the papal autocracy "thunder[s]" forth from her spiritual tower to daunt "Brute rapine"; and in the Roman Church, "Chastity finds many a sheltering bower." In sonnet II.28, the attenuation of the supremacy of papal power is spoken of in these terms:

> Grant, that by this unsparing hurricane
> Green leaves with yellow mixed are torn away,
> And goodly fruitage with the mother-spray.

The clearest example is in sonnet II.10, in which the Church is transformed into one of the poet's many tree images:

> Where long and deeply hath been fixed the root
> In the blest soil of gospel truth, the Tree,
> (Blighted or scathed though many branches be,
> Put forth to wither, many a hopeful shoot)
> Can never cease to bear celestial fruit.

Aside from resonating on the biblical association between tree and cross and on strains from Isaiah 11:1 ("And there shall come forth a rod out of the stem of Jesse, and a Branch shall grow out of his roots"), the tree imagery recalls sonnet I.21 on the war-weary chieftain and sonnet I.27 on Alfred's line of descendants.

So, while nature imagery in Part I has been used in relation to the Church, particularly to Christianity and faith, Part II endows the Church with beneficial characteristics of the natural world, thereby, at least temporarily, identifying one with the other.

The merging of humanity and nature either by comparing or identifying people with animals, especially birds (sonnets I.7, I.15, I.16, II.7, II.14, II.37, and II.45), or humanity's sin, for instance, with weeds (sonnets I.17, II.1, II.37, and III.20), carries over into Part II. But an interesting reversal in the approach occurs in sonnet II.4, in which an analogy between humanity and the natural world is used to argue for a distinction between them:

> Deplorable his lot who tills the ground,
> His whole life long tills it, with heartless toil
> Of villain-service, passing with the soil
> To each new Master, like a steer or hound
> Or like a rooted tree, or stone earth-bound.

This argument does not negate the value of the merging of humanity and nature in the series so far, or for that matter, in other works such as "The Leechgatherer" or the Lucy poems. The use of metaphorical merging to argue for distinction is a rhetorical reflection of the dynamic character of the poet's synthetic vision. Analytic powers, the ability to recognize and to shift the boundaries of categories, and the appreciation of uniqueness are processes inherent in the achievement and maintenance of a unified worldview. An ongoing, irreversible coalescence of elements, wherein similarity or interdependence would dissolve eventually into identification, would result in a worldview that resembled primordial slime. The poet's vision actively and operationally seeks similitude in dissimilitude and vice versa.

At the conclusion of Part II, nature and God are for the first time in the series overtly merged; previously, the presentation had been more subtle, with nature bonding with divinity.

Sonnet II.46, "Afflictions of England," uses similes to compare the ways of God with elements of the natural world: "like the firmament his ways: / His statutes like the chambers of the deep." This comparison echoes that of Psalm 36:5–6:

> Thy mercy, O Lord, is in the heavens; and thy faithfulness
>   reacheth unto the clouds.
> Thy righteousness is like the great mountains; thy judgments
>   are a great deep: O Lord, thou preservest man and beast.

The placement of this sonnet with this bonding at a narrative conclusion that laments the religious and political turmoil surrounding the end of the reign of Charles I, compellingly articulates nature as the foundational context for humanity's faith and guidance. In nature, first principles are manifested and God communicates in ways comprehensible to humanity.

Nature as God's medium is not new to the series (for instance, see sonnet II.39), and certainly not to Wordsworth's poetry, but the poet's call for a return to first principles through an overt coalescence of biblical history with the elements of a classical Wordsworthian landscape, including music and an echo, is notable. This coalescence is illustrated in sonnet II.46:

> Harp! couldst thou venture, on thy boldest string,
> The faintest note to echo which the blast
> Caught from the hand of Moses as it passed
> O'er Sinai's top, or from the Shepherd-king,
> Early awake, by Siloa's brook, to sing
> Of dread Jehovah; then, should wood and waste
> Hear also of that name, and mercy cast
> Off to the mountains, like a covering
> Of which the Lord was weary. Weep, oh! weep,
> Weep with the good, beholding King and Priest
> Despised by that stern God to whom they raise
> Their suppliant hands; but holy is the feast
> He keepeth; like the firmament his ways:
> His statutes like the chambers of the deep.

An intimation of the synthesis, so boldly set forth in this concluding sonnet, is offered by sonnets II.43 and II.44, which draw a striking analogy between a scene in nature and an unfortunate development in religion at this point in the historical narrative. Sonnet II.43, "Illustration: The Jung-Frau and the fall of the Rhine near Schaffhausen," contrasts the serene stately beauty of a snow-covered mountain with its extraordinary offspring—a raging waterfall, monstrous in its ferocity, deafening in its noise. The nature imagery is dominated by the generative character of water imagery, which relates importantly to the central image of the series, the Holy River; but also interesting is the distinct contrast in rhythm in this sonnet that imitates the intensity of the scene:

> The Virgin-Mountain, wearing like a Queen
> A brilliant crown of everlasting snow,
> Sheds ruin from her sides; and men below
> Wonder that aught of aspect so serene
> Can link with desolation. Smooth and green,
> And seeming, at a little distance, slow,
> The waters of the Rhine; but on they go
> Fretting and whitening, keener and more keen;
> Till madness seizes on the whole wide Flood,
> Turned to a fearful Thing whose nostrils breathe
> Blasts of tempestuous smoke—wherewith he tries
> To hide himself, but only magnifies;
> And doth in more conspicuous torment writhe,
> Deafening the region in his ireful mood.

The contrasting character of the mountain and its waterfall is compared in sonnet II.44, "Troubles of Charles the First," to piety and its perverted offspring, fanaticism. Nature imagery serves in this sonnet as a metaphorical context:

> Even such the contrast that, where'er we move,
> To the mind's eye Religion doth present;
> Now with her own deep quietness content;
> Then, like the mountain, thundering from above
> Against the ancient pine-trees of the grove
> And the Land's humblest comforts. Now her mood
> Recalls the transformation of the flood,
> Whose rage the gentle skies in vain reprove,
> Earth cannot check. O terrible excess

Of headstrong will! Can this be Piety?
No—some fierce Maniac hath usurped her name;
And scourges England struggling to be free:
Her peace destroyed! her hopes a wilderness!
Her blessings cursed—her glory turned to shame!

These two sonnets demonstrate the poet's exquisite, though here not subtle, integration of the human drama with the natural world and the value of the latter in helping humanity to make sense, even if only by analogy, of the all too common grotesque in human history.

Finally, it is worth noting that the emphasis in Part II on a synthetic vision that interfuses the boundaries of traditionally distinct concepts of humanity, Church, nature, and God is reflected in three sonnets strategically placed at the beginning, middle, and end of this part—sonnets II.1, II.21, and II.46. Sonnet II.1, following the bitter attack on the Roman Church in Part I, calls for "Charity" even in the sternest judgment. Sonnet II.21 manifests nature's healing and forgiveness of the wounds inflicted on the spiritual and literal landscape by the destruction of the monasteries. Sonnet II.46 offers a stabilizing perspective on a period of political and religious turmoil by calling forth the first principles manifested in the relationship between nature and God. These three sonnets of Part II represent a vital closure of the wounds necessarily reopened by the poet's courageous journey through the communal Christian past, in his attempt to come to terms with his Christian identity within the collective experience of the struggle with faith and service in the fallen world.

8

Part III: Toward the Apocalypse—
The New Eden in the Fallen World

The historical narrative of Part III selectively examines almost
160 years, from the Restoration in 1660 to 1818, when Parliament voted one million pounds for the building of new
churches in England. Even if the reader's knowledge of the
historical background is minimal, Part III remains accessible
because it is least dependent upon historical events, with only
fourteen strongly historical sonnets. The historical events upon
which these sonnets are based are more recent (including a set
of three sonnets entitled "Aspects of Christianity in America"),
which further facilitates the reading of Part III. Fifteen sonnets
(III.19 to III.33) are about religious ceremonies: baptism, confirmation, marriage, and funeral, familiar to almost any reader.
Another group of ten sonnets (III.17, III.35, and III.38 to 45)
is devoted to places of worship: old abbeys, new churches,
and cathedrals (including three on King's College Chapel,
Cambridge).

Of the remaining twenty-two sonnets in Part III, eight lend
themselves to be read independently of the series. Sonnet
III.1, "I saw the figure of a lovely Maid," on Wordsworth's
daughter Dora, is one of only three overtly biographical sonnets in the series. Sonnet III.2, "Patriotic sympathies," can be
read in conjunction with the previous sonnet because it addresses the concept of filial love that joins love of family with

love of country. Sonnet III.12, "Down a swift Stream, thus far, a bold design," an earlier version of which appeared in the 1822 edition of *Memorials of a Tour of the Continent*, mingles the landscape of the Rhine with the landscape of memory, first interweaving then transcending the time/space continuum. Sonnet III.16, "Bishops and Priests, blessed are ye, if deep," focuses on clerical responsibility. Sonnet III.18, "Pastoral character," is a finely inspired, energetic observation of the role of the pastor in the community. Sonnet III.34, "Mutability," is a beautiful song about the outward forms of truth. Sonnet III.46, "Ejaculation," interplays light and dark imagery reminiscent of the Gospel according to St. John, Wordsworth's favorite book of the Bible. Sonnet III.47, "Conclusion," interweaves the power of the Word, both divine and poetic, with the water imagery of the Holy River of time—past, present, and future—an excellent sonnet to pair with the concluding *Duddon* sonnet, "After-thought," which merges the image of a river with the concepts of eternality, death, and meaningfulness. [1]

Autobiographical material extends the time span to 1820, when the poet and Sir George Beaumont walked through Beaumont's estate at Coleorton to select a site for a church. This undertaking brought forth sonnets III.39, III.40, and III.41, which were the beginning of what was known from 1822 to 1837 as the *Ecclesiastical Sketches*.

There are five narrative sections to Part III. The first section, sonnets III.1 to III.11, actually concludes the series' fast-paced historical account of the Church in Britain with attention to the political and religious concerns of individual conscience, toleration, and High and Low Church tensions. The major historical figures of this section are Charles II, Milton, William III, Algernon Sidney and William Russell, Henry Sacheverel, and Bishop White.

Sonnet III.12, a transitional sonnet that functions like the deliberately ambiguous beginnings and endings of phrases in Bach, both concludes the first group and introduces the second. It is a retrospective upon the whole of the series—that "bold design" of a journey "Down a swift Stream," during which "living landscapes" quickly rise and fall. But sonnet

III.12 declares a respite from our having "hurried on with troubled pleasure," and alters the series' mood:

> Henceforth, as on the bosom of a stream
> That slackens, and spreads wide a watery gleam,
> We, nothing loth a lingering course to measure,
> May gather up our thoughts, and mark at leisure
> How widely spread the interests of our theme.

As a key transitional sonnet in Part III and the series as a whole, this sonnet also breathes fresh life into the series' central river symbol with the stream images and their associations with thought and time.

Sonnet III.12 could be viewed as beginning the second group of sonnets, which advances in a historical, digressive fashion to sonnet III.18. Sonnets III.13 to III.15 are historical in that they address the role of the Anglican (Episcopal) Church in America, yet they digress from the established historical account of the Church in Britain. Sonnets III.16 to III.18, articulating the responsibility of clergy and the influence and role of the church building in the community, arise tangentially from the previous sonnets and introduce, through association, the next major section, which is on the liturgy. Sonnet III.17, "Places of worship," also serves as a precursor to the fourth section on churches.

The third section, sonnets III.19 to III.33, examines the liturgy: baptism and the role of godparents, recitation of the catechism, confirmation, the Eucharist, marriage, thanksgiving after childbirth, visitation of the sick, commination service, forms of prayer at sea, funeral services, and the Rushbearing ceremony (peculiar to churches in Westmoreland). The sonnets on the rituals of the Church introduce a different mood and character to the series. Because these rituals serve into the twentieth century, the reader's assimilation of them is direct, eliminating any effort to translate them through time or vicarious experience. These sonnets are particularly easy to read and relate to, and many are remarkably beautiful.

The fourth section, sonnets III.34 to III.45, begins with

the celebrated sonnet "Mutability" and relates old and new churches, especially their architectural components, even if in ruins, to their spiritual impress. The nature imagery in this section is distinguished by a dramatic complement of sound imagery, particularly music and echoes.

The final section, sonnets III.46 and III.47, though it does not employ music imagery, manifests a symphonic closure to the series with a bold oratorical finale. Sonnet III.46 glories in its amalgam of humanity, Christ, and nature: Christ merges divinity with humanity, and he is described with a series of analogies to nature. In the concluding sonnet, also empowered by nature imagery, the central image of the Holy River makes a spectacular final appearance as a symbol of Christian faith through time past, when it suddenly bursts through the inert present into the apocalyptic future.

The structure of this chapter reflects, rather than this narrative organization, the concluding character of Part III, which reviews the dynamic nature of the poet's synthetic vision manifested in the interactive penetration of the spiritual and phenomenal worlds. As to the interfacing of nature and the Church, Part III adds a new feature: the impress on the literal and psychological landscape from the incorporation of the church building into nature. Part III also continues the intriguing shift begun in Part II from nature typically serving as a context for the Church to the Church appropriating nature and some of nature's roles. Furthermore, Part III intensifies and modulates the ongoing integration of humanity and nature by orchestrating a rousing finale that highlights the merger of humanity and God in Christ and links Christ's image and service with the landscape. And time, which has been an insidious presence throughout the series, primarily in the effort to transcend it, here emerges thematically and is personified, particularly from sonnet III.34 to the conclusion, where Time is ultimately subjugated by a prophetic apocalyptic vision. This chapter discusses a selection of sonnets from Part III, combining them into four groups: the Church and the landscape, the Church's assimilation of nature, humanity and nature, and time and nature.

Sonnets III.17, III.18, and III.39 to III.41:
The Literal and Symbolic Integration of the Church
into the Landscape

Sonnets III.39 to III.41 represent the birth of the series and
arose from Wordsworth's helping Sir George Beaumont select
a site for a church at Coleorton. That they arise from the poet's
concern for integrating the church building and its symbolic
value into the landscape is a fitting and significant inception
for this major work of 132 sonnets that details the intellectual
and spiritual journey through which the poet endeavors to
assimilate the collective Christian past. The series begins in
the attempt to integrate a church building into the landscape
and continues in the ongoing endeavor to integrate the history
of Christianity in Britain, and Christianity itself, with the
expansive concept of nature and the life and faith of the individual.

The integration of the church into the landscape, concen-
trated in sonnets III.39 to III.41, is introduced in sonnet
III.38 with the image of "channels" shaped by the state for the
"Flood / Of sacred truth," referring to the one million pounds
voted by Parliament in 1818 for the building of new churches.
The sonnet concludes by merging the churches into the landscape through the music of church bells:

> the wished-for Temples rise!
> I hear their sabbath bells' harmonious chime
> Float on the breeze—the heavenliest of all sounds
> That vale or hill prolongs or multiplies!

The receptivity and cooperation of nature is seen in the breeze
carrying the sound and in the vale or hill, not merely passively
echoing, but "prolong[ing]" and "multipl[ying]" the sound.
The word choice assigns to nature an active, participatory role
in incorporating the church's physical presence and its spiritual
service to humanity.

This active cooperation operates overtly in sonnets III.39
and III.40. In sonnet III.39, although the "virgin sod" seems
rather passively to disappear, the "grateful earth receive[s] /

The corner-stone from hands that build to God" and "forest oaks . . . shelter the Abode / Of genuine Faith." And in return, merging nature and religion, the "mystic Dove," "visibly portrayed," protects the land from blasphemy. In sonnet III.40, nature is active again. The first rays of the sun "greet" the cross that crowns the church and

> the fresh air of incense-breathing morn
> Shall wooingly embrace it; and green moss
> Creep round its arms through centuries unborn.

The anthropomorphizing of nature in its seemingly conscious and willing acceptance of the Church and its role is intensified in the poet's concept of landscape with its own memory. In sonnet III.39, for instance, the linking of nature with human experience leaves a record not only in the human mind, but also in nature, which is endowed with memory through its participatory experience with humanity:

> Those forest oaks of Druid memory,
> Shall long survive, to shelter the Abode
> Of genuine Faith. Where, haply, 'mid this band
> Of daisies, shepherds sate of yore and wove
> May-garlands, there let the holy altar stand
> For kneeling adoration.

In sonnet III.41, which describes the transformation of native turf to churchyard, the memory of the "rugged colts" playing and the "wild deer bound[ing] through the forest glade, / Unchecked as when by merry Outlaw driven" seems at first to be a human recollection. But in the next lines, the land itself feels and remembers:

> And soon, full soon, the lonely Sexton's spade
> Shall wound the tender sod. Encincture small,
> But infinite its grasp of weal and woe!

Nature participates in human life and shares the suffering and loss as well as the drive toward the manifestation of its divinity. The close of this sonnet, if viewed in isolation, speaks of and

from a human perspective, but within the context generated
by the previous three sonnets, the cycle of human endeavor is
absorbed into a coherent infrastructure of nature and Church:

> Hopes, fears, in never-ending ebb and flow;—
> The spousal trembling, and the "dust to dust,"
> The prayers, the contrite struggle, and the trust
> That to the Almighty Father looks through all.
>   (III.41)

The Church in its symbiotic relationship with nature may serve
as a center around which humanity (as a society) and the
individual (in the wholeness of selfhood) can move closer to a
recognition of a divine internal presence and potential for
goodness and service.

The integration of the Church and its architecture into the
landscape is presented more subtly in sonnets III.17 and
III.18. Sonnet III.17 establishes a set of analogies that highlights the interdependency of elements in the landscape and
the interdependency of nature and human experience:

> As star that shines dependent upon star
> Is to the sky while we look up in love;
> As to the deep fair ships which though they move
> Seem fixed, to eyes that watch them from afar;
> As to the sandy desert fountains are,
> With palm-groves shaded at wide intervals,
> Whose fruit around the sun-burnt Native falls
> Of roving tired or desultory war—
> Such to this British Isle her Christian Fanes.

This network links elements of nature (stars, sky, desert, fountain, fruit) to humanity individually and collectively (ships,
"eyes that watch," "sun-burnt Native," the "British Isle," and
"Christian Fanes").

This complex interconnection is then interfaced with the
relationship among Christian churches in Britain and their
relationship with the landscape and with humanity:

> Each linked to each for kindred services;
> Her Spires, her Steeple-towers with glittering vanes
> Far-kenned, her Chapels lurking among trees,
> Where a few villagers on bended knees
> Find solace which a busy world disdains.
>
> (III.17)

Nature and the Church (both in its religious role and through its aesthetic influence) cooperatively offer consolation and renewal in the fallen world.

Sonnet III.18 and Wordsworth's note to the sonnet unite the valuable role of the pastor living among his flock with the beneficial impress of the parsonage, church, and graveyard on the literal and psychological landscape of people's daily lives. The pastor, though "meek," "patient," humble, and a model of "civility and refinement" (Wordsworth's note), is also "arrayed in Christ's authority," and as such:

> He from the pulpit lifts his awful hand;
> Conjures, implores, and labours all he can
> For re-subjecting to divine command
> The stubborn spirit of rebellious man.

The pastor's attempt to recall wandering souls to sympathy is reinforced by the harmonious acceptance of the church building, graveyard, and parsonage into the landscape. The familiar scene becomes a symbolic gesture, a persistent subliminal reminder of the synthesis of nature, humanity, and divine spirit. Wordsworth's note to the sonnet reads in part: "A parsonage-house generally stands not far from the church; this proximity imposes favourable restraints, and sometimes suggests an affecting union of the accommodations and elegancies of life with the outward signs of piety and mortality."

The latter part of this note describes a particular parsonage and churchyard, "in the residence of an old and much-valued friend in Oxfordshire," the details of which highlight the scene's role as a daily reminder of the interpenetration of nature, human life, and faith:

> The house and church stand parallel to each other, at a small distance; a circular lawn, or rather grass-plot, spreads between

them; shrubs and trees curve from each side of the dwelling, veiling, but not hiding, the church. From the front of this dwelling no part of the burial-ground is seen; but as you wind by the side of the shrubs towards the steeple-end of the church, the eye catches a single, small, low, monumental head-stone, moss-grown, sinking into, and gently inclining towards the earth. Advance, and the churchyard, populous and gay with glittering tombstones, opens upon the view.[2]

These sonnets are a partial testimony to a distinct Edenistic impetus in Wordsworth's poetry. Although his portrayal of human tragedy evidences his full awareness of the fallen nature of the world, the talismanic spots of both time and place in the natural world testify to the poet's belief in the possibility of a retrieval of that sense of the unfallen state—moments in which connection with the divinity is unattenuated by reminders of imperfection and division—extraordinary moments perceived as above time, without past or future; a transcendent state in which selfhood dissipates and participation in the divine being is not rationally cognized, but spiritually discerned.

Sonnets III.20, III.33, III.38, and III.43 to III.45:
The Integration of Nature into the Church

The dynamic character of the poet's conception of the interpenetration of nature and the Church is evidenced in the reciprocal functions of nature and the Church as contexts. The spatial and psychological contexts, usually ascribed to nature, are transferred to the Church in such a way that nature and the Church coalesce.

The most literal assimilation of nature by the Church is offered in sonnet III.33, in which the church building, filled with greens at Christmas, serves as a "counter Spirit" to nature in winter:

Go, seek, when Christmas snows discomfort bring,
The counter Spirit found in some gay church
Green with fresh holly, every pew a perch
In which the linnet or the thrush might sing,
Merry and loud and safe from prying search,
Strains offered only to the genial Spring.

The Church's rituals comfort those suffering from the burdens of life in the fallen world and offer renewed energy and hope. Sonnet III.33 shows the poet's regret for the scarcity of "those graceful rites" (such as the Rushbearing ceremony described in sonnet III.32), that cause

> A stir of mind too natural to deceive;
> Giving to Memory help when she would weave
> A crown for Hope!

The power of sensual aspects of the natural scene that in Wordsworth's poetry traditionally prompt association and memory, moving to enlightened states of mind, is now transferred to the Church. Light and dark, sound (music and echoes), and spots of precious time are now generated by humanity's experience of the Church. In sonnet III.43, "Inside of King's College Chapel, Cambridge," for instance, the architecture calls forth a state of perception typically associated with the contemplation of nature:

> These lofty pillars, spread that branching roof
> Self-poised, and scooped into ten thousand cells,
> Where light and shade repose, where music dwells
> Lingering—and wandering on as loth to die;
> Like thoughts whose very sweetness yieldeth proof
> That they were born for immortality.

In sonnet III.44, the sensual play of light and dark, music and echoes, moves the parishioner to "ecstasy":

> What awful pérspective! while from our sight
> With gradual stealth the lateral windows hide
> Their Portraitures, their stone-work glimmers, dyed
> In the soft chequerings of a sleepy light.
> Martyr, or King, or sainted Eremite,
> Whoe'er ye be, that thus, yourselves unseen,
> Imbue your prison-bars with solemn sheen,
> Shine on, until ye fade with coming Night!—
> But, from the arms of silence—list! O list!
> The music bursteth into second life;
> The notes luxuriate, every stone is kissed

> By sound, or ghost of sound, in mazy strife;
> Heart-thrilling strains, that cast, before the eye
> Of the devout, a veil of ecstasy!

The echo, a key feature in the integration of nature and the Church throughout the series (recall particularly the Hallelujah Victory in sonnet I.11, and the echo to the call for the crusades in sonnet I.33) is shared in Part III by nature and the Church. In sonnet III.38 "New churches," the "Temples rise" and nature participates in the celebration:

> I hear their sabbath bells' harmonious chime
> Float on the breeze—the heavenliest of all sounds
> That vale or hill prolongs or multiplies!

Perhaps the most striking use of an echo occurs in sonnet III.20, "Baptism," in which the infant's cry, echoing in the tombs, serves as a reminder of his resurrection, "his second birth":

> Dear be the Church that, watching o'er the needs
> Of Infancy, provides a timely shower
> Whose virtue changes to a Christian Flower
> A Growth from sinful Nature's bed of weeds!—
> Fitliest beneath the sacred roof proceeds
> The ministration; while parental Love
> Looks on, and Grace descendeth from above
> As the high service pledges now, now pleads.
> There, should vain thoughts outspread their wings and fly
> To meet the coming hours of festal mirth,
> The tombs—which hear and answer that brief cry,
> The Infant's notice of his second birth—
> Recall the wandering Soul to sympathy
> With what man hopes from Heaven, yet fears from Earth.

This use of the echo is reminiscent of Wordsworth's 1806 poem, "Yes, It Was the Mountain Echo," which uses the mountain's reply to the cuckoo to demonstrate how the echo, through the original sound's interaction with nature, can take on more significance than the original utterance:

—yes, we have
Answers, and we know not whence;
Echoes from beyond the grave,
Recognized intelligence!

Such rebounds our inward ear
Catches sometimes from afar—
Listen, ponder, hold them dear;
For of God,—of God they are.
                                        (13–20)

In sonnet III.45, the mystical experiences usually prompted by nature are generated by King's College Chapel, Westminster Abbey, and St. Paul's Cathedral:

They dreamt not of a perishable home
Who thus could build. Be mine, in hours of fear
Or grovelling thought, to seek a refuge here;
Or through the aisles of Westminster to roam;
Where bubbles burst, and folly's dancing foam
Melts, if it cross the threshold; where the wreath
Of awe-struck wisdom droops: or let my path
Lead to that younger Pile, whose sky-like dome
Hath typified by reach of daring art
Infinity's embrace; whose guardian crest,
The silent Cross, among the stars shall spread
As now, when She hath also seen her breast
Filled with mementos, satiate with its part
Of grateful England's overflowing Dead.

Sonnets III.1 and III.20 to III.24: The Integration of Humanity into Nature

Continuing to demonstrate the various features of the poet's synthetic vision, Part III provides several sonnets that overtly integrate humanity with nature and the landscape, the most important of which are III.1 and III.20 to III.22. Two of these, sonnets III.1 and III.22, are autobiographical, the first relating to the poet's daughter Dora, the second to his mother, Ann. Sonnets III.20 and III.21 address the service of baptism and the duty of godparents. These four sonnets, and indeed the

two that follow, are interwoven with vegetation imagery, while
sonnets III.20 to III.22 are further interwoven with flower
imagery.

The first sonnet in Part III, one of the most beautiful sonnets
of the series, describes an actual dream Wordsworth had of
his daughter Dora. The sonnet, while visually beautiful, is a
parent's nightmare. The father envisions Dora, then about
seventeen, a lovely, bright image sitting in the shade of a
"fondly-overhanging" tree. But as he gazes, her image gradually dissolves into a "sunny mist" and finally into thin air:

> I saw the figure of a lovely Maid
> Seated alone beneath a darksome tree,
> Whose fondly-overhanging canopy
> Set off her brightness with a pleasing shade.
> No Spirit was she; *that* my heart betrayed,
> For she was one I loved exceedingly;
> But while I gazed in tender reverie
> (Or was it sleep that with my Fancy played?)
> The bright corporeal presence—form and face—
> Remaining still distinct grew thin and rare,
> Like sunny mist;—at length the golden hair,
> Shape, limbs, and heavenly features, keeping pace
> Each with the other in a lingering race
> Of dissolution, melted into air.[3]

The poet relates the dream to his agonized concerns for the
welfare of his country ("I partake / Of kindred agitations for
thy sake," sonnet III.2).[4] But the poet's fears about the loss of
Dora must have been associated with and reinforced by his
loss of Catharine (aged four) and Thomas (aged six) in 1812.
The dream also grotesquely predicts that the poet was in fact
to endure the loss of his beloved Dora, who died in 1847 at
the age of forty-three. Harper describes this as "the greatest
affliction of his life. . . . From this blow he never recovered."[5]
The sonnet testifies, however, to the tenacity of his attachment
to his synthetic vision; for even in a "Vision [that] spake / Fear
into [his] Soul" (III.2), nature and humanity coalesce, which
recalls the imagery of the Lucy poems.[6]

The absorption of the loved one into nature takes on special significance in sonnet III.20, "Baptism," in which the effects of the Fall are suffered by both humanity and nature; however, nature, at least symbolically, also benefits from the effects of grace. The rite of baptism takes "A Growth from sinful Nature's bed of weeds" and converts it to "a Christian Flower."[7] And in sonnet III.21, the godparents tend the "adopted Plant" so that it "may thrive / For everlasting bloom."

Although the vision of Dora dissolves into a sunny mist, nature imagery also returns life. Flowers in sonnets III.20 and III.21 are associated with Christ's saving grace and the promise of eternal life. And in sonnet III.22, flowers actually resurrect the memory of the face of Wordsworth's mother, even though she died in 1778, when he was only seven:

> Belovèd Mother! Thou whose happy hand
> Had bound the flowers I wore, with faithful tie:
> Sweet flowers! at whose inaudible command
> Her countenance, phantom-like, doth reappear:
> O lost too early for the frequent tear,
> And ill requited by this heartfelt sigh!

As the poet recounts: "I remember my mother only in some few situations, one of which was her pinning a nosegay to my breast when I was going to say the Catechism in the church, as was customary before Easter."[8]

Perhaps some motivation for the writing of the *Ecclesiastical Sonnets* lies in this rare memory of his mother, associated with a church service, particularly at Easter, with the anxious responsibility of having to recite the catechism. Her early loss, and that of his father five years later, must have been borne with patient strength fortified by faith.

Sonnets III.23 and III.24, on confirmation, are thematically linked to the sonnets that deal with significant loss. Sonnet III.23, "Confirmation," addresses the loss of childhood, merging the loss with nature, so that childhood sets like the sun ("ere the Sun goes down their childhood sets"). In sonnet III.24, "Confirmation continued," a mother is reminded of the death of one of her children as she witnesses the confirmation of a surviving daughter:

Tell what rushed in, from what she was relieved—
Then, when her Child the hallowing touch received,
And such vibration through the Mother went
That tears burst forth amain. Did gleams appear?
Opened a vision of that blissful place
Where dwells a Sister-child? And was power given
Part of her lost One's glory back to trace
Even to this Rite? For thus *She* knelt, and, ere
The summer-leaf had faded, passed to Heaven.

All experience is connected, each experience tracing back to another through memory and association; but in the poet's vision, all experience is somehow connected to, measured by, and remembered through nature. The coherence of the vision pulsates throughout the series and the oeuvre. *The Prelude* proclaims that "Nature's self . . . is the breath of God" (1805.V.222).

The climax of humanity's integration into nature comes in sonnet III.46, in which Christ's form and function, representing the coalescence of God and humanity, merges with the landscape through a series of analogies that culminates in a play on Son/Sun:

Glory to God! and to the Power who came
In filial duty, clothed with love divine,
That made His human tabernacle shine
Like Ocean burning with purpureal flame;
Or like the Alpine Mount, that takes its name
From roseate hues, far kenned at morn and even,
In hours of peace, or when the storm is driven
Along the nether region's rugged frame!
Earth prompts—Heaven urges; let us seek the light,
Studious of that pure intercourse begun
When first our infant brows their lustre won;
So, like the Mountain, may we grow more bright
From unimpeded commerce with the Sun,
At the approach of all-involving night.

The poet nurtures a synthetic philosophical vision that perceives and creates a dynamic context in which the ostensibly separate phenomenological and spiritual worlds actively merge. In this generative interplay, traditional Western categories of existence speak not only of themselves but also of one another, so that what is sensual is also spiritual, what is other is also self, and what is past is also present and future.

Sonnets III.12, III.19, III.34, and III.47:
The Integration of Time into Nature

For Wordsworth, life with its joys and sufferings is comprehended and borne in its interrelationship to nature. As Part III demonstrates nature's incorporation of the Church and human experience, it also shows, perhaps more strongly than either Part I or Part II, that nature also serves as a context for time. But finally, this interaction fuses and there is neither time nor nature. Four sonnets serve to demonstrate the relationship between time and nature in Part III: nature as a measure of time in sonnets III.12 and III.34, and the apocalyptic relationship between time and nature in sonnets III.19 and III.47.

Sonnet III.12 returns to the central image of the series, the Holy River, the river as history, merging nature and human experience over time. This sonnet articulates what the reader has already gleaned: there are "living landscapes" that are alive with human life and with such a vital memory of human life and its interaction with nature that the record is not housed in the human mind but as a pulsating, breathing memory belonging to the landscape itself. Significantly, the process along this "swift Stream" is measured in the rising and sinking of church spires. This process overtly integrates nature, the Church, and human experience—an integration heretofore more obliquely evolved in the series. This sonnet, in keeping with the role of the Holy River, associates the "Stream" not only with the journey through time, but also with the individual's assimilation of the meaning of past human experience. The pace of the river is slowed so that the smooth reflection of the water's surface is likened to our "gather[ing] up our thoughts" on what the poet and reader have experienced in the trek through the Christian past:

Down a swift Stream, thus far, a bold design
Have we pursued, with livelier stir of heart
Than his who sees, borne forward by the Rhine,
The living landscapes greet him, and depart;
Sees spires fast sinking—up again to start!
And strives the towers to number, that recline
O'er the dark steeps, or on the horizon line
Striding with shattered crests his eye athwart.
So have we hurried on with troubled pleasure:
Henceforth, as on the bosom of a stream
That slackens, and spreads wide a watery gleam,
We, nothing loth a lingering course to measure,
May gather up our thoughts, and mark at leisure
How widely spread the interests of our theme.

The well-known sonnet III.34, "Mutability," merges sound and nature as manifestations of time:

From low to high doth dissolution climb,
And sink from high to low, along a scale
Of awful notes, whose concord shall not fail;
A musical but melancholy chime,
Which they can hear who meddle not with crime,
Nor avarice, nor over-anxious care.
Truth fails not; but her outward forms that bear
The longest date do melt like frosty rime,
That in the morning whitened hill and plain
And is no more; drop like the tower sublime
Of yesterday, which royally did wear
His crown of weeds, but could not even sustain
Some casual shout that broke the silent air,
Or the unimaginable touch of Time.

What appear to be changes over time are but notes of a scale, whose harmony prevails for those who can hear it. But the outward forms of Truth melt like frost, and man's labor ("tower sublime") in the fallen world ("weeds") is undone by the "casual shout" of another or by "the unimaginable touch of Time" itself. The conclusion of this sonnet, with Time personified, with its touch awesomely dropping the sublime ruin of a tower to the ground, challenges the reader first to perceive time as a measurable reality and also as a construct of the imagination and then to unite both in a coherent vision. It is a challenge at which Western thought balks.

Time personified appears twice in the next sonnet: first, in the course of our lives we are "made wise" and tolerant "by the discipline of Time" and second, in relation to old abbeys:

> Why should we break Time's charitable seals?
> Once ye were holy, ye are holy still;
> Your spirit freely let me drink, and live.
>
> (III.35)

While the spiritual accepts mutability as evidence of linear time, it transcends linear time by encompassing Time. In other words, the spiritual becomes a context for Time, not a function of it.

The connection between this mutability and changelessness is symbolized in the circle, which figures in sonnet III.19. The "signs" in nature and in the church calendar seem to indicate a linear progression through time, but the progression is only a circle repeated in the cycles of the seasons and in the Church calendar from the celebration of Advent through the celebration of the Resurrection. There is a larger cycle, however: "Upon that circle traced from sacred story / We only dare to cast a transient glance." Although the poet uses the word "circle," the reference is to that progression from Genesis to Revelation, here measured from Christ's birth to his Second Coming: "From his mild advent till his countenance / Shall dissipate the seas and mountains hoary." In one way this sonnet reasserts time, and in another, destroys it.

The conclusion of the series asserts Wordsworth's particular apocalyptic vision that postulates a potential return to a modified Edenistic state previous to the prophesied apocalyptic destruction. The sonnet ingeniously recalls Genesis with the image of the snake, but here a "snake enrolled," sleeping, represents the future that seems to undo the Fall:

> Why sleeps the future, as a snake enrolled,
> Coil within coil, at noon-tide? For the WORD
> Yields, if with unpresumptuous faith explored,

Power at whose touch the sluggard shall unfold
His drowsy rings. Look forth!—that Stream behold,
THAT STREAM upon whose bosom we have passed
Floating at ease while nations have effaced
Nations, and Death has gathered to his fold
Long lines of mighty Kings—look forth, my Soul!
(Nor in this vision be thou slow to trust)
The living Waters, less and less by guilt
Stained and polluted, brighten as they roll,
Till they have reached the eternal City—built
For the perfécted Spirits of the just!

                                                        (III.47)

The Stream that has persisted despite the mutability of "Nations effac[ing] Nations" and the deaths of "mighty Kings," still
flows, purifying itself. It is given life and power as "living
Waters," in conjunction with the "living landscapes" in sonnet
III.12. The persistently significant and active role of nature
in these key theological sonnets asserts the poet's belief in
humanity's potential to achieve, through an active synthetic
vision, a way of life, a manner of thought, that approximates
a blessedness and well-being reminiscent of a prelapsarian
state. This Edenistic vision excludes any remnant of naivete;
the comprehensiveness of his perception resists blindness to
suffering and perverse circumstances.

His Edenistic vision, without rejecting the prophecy of Revelation, modulates it—the world need not get worse before
the Second Coming but better. The judgment may not and
need not take the form of nearly wholesale damnation. His
vision provides for the possible avoidance of Armageddon and
a new definition of apocalypse that, although it does away with
the world as we know it, creates a new one based on the
operation of the divine potential latent in humanity at present.
His poetry posits a God that so loves nature and humanity that
he would be loath to destroy it. This vision of the interpenetration of God with his creation manifests an eschatological triumph of affirmation, a vision of paradise regained, in which
harmony reigns:

    And there shall come forth a rod out of the stem of Jesse, and a
    Branch shall grow out of his roots: and the spirit of the Lord

shall rest upon him, the spirit of wisdom and understanding, the spirit of counsel and might, the spirit of the knowledge and of the fear of the Lord. . . . The wolf. . . shall dwell with the lamb, and the leopard shall lie down with the kid; and the calf and the young lion and the fatling together; and a little child shall lead them. And the cow and the bear shall feed; their young ones shall lie down together; and the lion shall eat straw like the ox. . . . They shall not hurt nor destroy in all my holy mountain: for the earth shall be full of the knowledge of the Lord, as the waters cover the sea. (Isaiah 11.1–2, 6–7, 9)

Appendixes

Notes

Selected Bibliography

Index

Appendix A:
List of Exclamations

These first-line exclamations, many of which are imperatives, lend immediacy to the sonnets.

I.6	Lament!
I.8	Watch, and be firm!
I.10	Rise!
I.16	"Man's life is like a Sparrow, mighty King!"
I.29	Woe to the Crown that doth the Cowl obey!
II.1	How soon—alas!
II.7	And what melodious sounds at times prevail!
II.11	Enough!
II.13	Praised be the Rivers!
II.18	"Woe to you, Prelates!"
II.25	Mother!
II.27	Deep is the lamentation!
II.34	How fast the Marian death-list is unrolled!
II.38	Hail, Virgin Queen!
II.46	Harp!
III.2I	Father!
III.27	Woman!
III.35	Monastic Domes!
III.42	Open your gates, ye everlasting Piles!
III.44	What awful pérspective!
III.46	Glory to God!

Appendix B:
The Hallelujah Victory

The following selection is from Book One, chapter 20 of Bede's *History of the English Church and People.*

Strong in faith and fresh from the waters of Baptism, the [British] army advanced; and whereas they had formerly despaired of human strength, all now trusted in the power of God. The preparation and disposition of the British forces was reported to the enemy, who, anticipating an easy victory over an ill-equipped army, advanced rapidly, closely observed by the British scouts.

After the Feast of Easter, when the greater part of the British forces, fresh from the font, were preparing to arm and embark on the struggle, Germanus promised to direct the battle in person. He picked out the most active men and, having surveyed the surrounding country, observed a valley among the hills lying in the direction from which he expected the enemy to approach. Here he stationed the untried forces under his own orders. By now the main body of their remorseless enemies was approaching, watched by those whom he had placed in ambush. Suddenly Germanus, raising the standard, called upon them all to join him in a mighty shout. While the enemy advanced confidently, expecting to take the Britons unawares, the bishops three times shouted, "Alleluia!" The whole army joined in this shout, until the surrounding hills echoed with the sound. The enemy column panicked, thinking that the very rocks and sky were falling on them, and were so terrified that they could not run fast enough. Throwing away their weapons in headlong flight, they were well content to escape naked, while many in their hasty flight were drowned in a river which they tried to cross. So the innocent British army saw its defeats avenged, and became an inactive spectator of the victory granted to it. The scattered spoils were collected, and the Christian forces rejoiced in the triumph of heaven. So the bishops overcame the enemy without bloodshed, winning a victory by faith and not by force.

Appendix C:
Early Evidence of Christianity in Britain

Working backwards through the evidence, according to Edwards' *Christian England,* in 359, three British bishops were offered reimbursement for expenses of travel abroad by the imperial treasury.[1] In 325, at a council called by Constantine (288?–337), the British are listed as accepting the orthodox beliefs defined by the council.[2] In 314, five British bishops[3] were present at the Council of Arles.[4] Also, there were Roman executions of Christians in Britain during the third century, as Wordsworth points out in sonnet I.6, "Persecution."[5] For the earliest possibilities, Neill asserts that Christianity traveled fast along the trade routes and with the army: "There would be nothing surprising in the presence of Christian soldiers on the Roman Wall in the second century A.D."[6] And Tertullian, writing in the early third century, claims that "parts of Britain inaccessible to the Romans were indeed conquered by Christ."[7] Furthermore, Glastonbury, inhabited in A.D. 1, when there was considerable traffic across the Channel, is said to have been the site of a wooden church, described by King Ine of the West Saxons in the seventh century as already ancient. This church was destroyed by fire in 1184.[8]

Notes

Introduction

1. On the originality of the idea of the *Ecclesiastical Sonnets*, see Mary Moorman, *William Wordsworth: A Biography* (New York: Oxford Univ. Press, 1965), 394, and George McLean Harper, *William Wordsworth: His Life, Works, and Influence* (New York: Scribner's, 1929), 573. The workmanship of each sonnet respects the integrity of the genre, and the beauty of the sonnets arises from inspired and sometimes relentless attention to detail. Lee M. Johnson writes:

> There are reasons of form . . . which suggest that Wordsworth aimed for perfection in his series. Several scholars have asserted that his later sonnets show a falling-off of craftsmanship in comparison with the earlier pieces, and that this carelessness of technique reflects the deterioration of his poetic abilities. This criticism is usually based on the extent of Wordsworth's fidelity to traditional models as the criterion of excellence. His later sonnets generally support this charge. The *Ecclesiastical Sonnets*, however, are a striking exception. (*Wordsworth and the Sonnet* [Copenhagen: Rosenkilde and Bagger, 1973], 168)

Harper writes:

> [The] criticism is less concerned with [Wordsworth's] limitations as an historian than with the degree on which he succeeded in turning history, or what was supposed to be history, into poetry. And here, I

115

think, he is to be highly praised. Some of the sonnets are pompous, some are mechanical; but a certain number show the hand of a consummate artist moulding into sensuous form lofty and passionately conceived thoughts (574).

2. The poet encourages the reader to seek a comprehensive overview of his works. In the 1814 preface to *The Excursion*, for instance, Wordsworth makes the following statement, which could be applied to his works in general, regarding the "system" inherent in *The Recluse:* "It is not the Author's intention formally to announce a system: it was more animating to him to proceed in a different course; and if he shall succeed in conveying to the mind clear thoughts, lively images, and strong feelings, the Reader will have no difficulty in extracting the system for himself" (John O. Hayden, ed. *William Wordsworth: The Poems*, 2 vols. [New Haven, Conn.: Yale Univ. Press, 1981], 1:37).

Frederika Beatty states that "no one who comes to know William Wordsworth can fail to feel the essential unity of his mind and work from first to last" (*William Wordsworth of Rydal Mount* [London: Dent, 1939], v). And Abbie Findley Potts argues that "if the *Ecclesiastical Sonnets* are to take their rightful place in a survey of Wordsworth's art, his career must be thought of as homogeneous; and this conception would be Wordsworth's own" (*The Ecclesiastical Sonnets of William Wordsworth: A Critical Edition* [New Haven, Conn.: Yale Univ. Press, 1922], 2).

3. Johnson writes, "It is simply the most thoroughly researched work he ever composed. It is a veritable bibliography of sources for English church history" (151). Moorman briefly discusses Wordsworth's sources (2:392–93), but the most thorough analysis is Potts' critical edition. See note 3, chapter 2 of the present study for a list of Wordsworth's main sources.

4. The Fenwick note states, "My purpose in writing this Series, was as much as possible, to confine my view to the introduction, progress, and operation of the Church in England, both previous and subsequent to the Reformation" (Hayden, 2:997).

Barbara T. Gates, overvaluing the Fenwick note and misconstruing the work's purpose, criticizes the series for being selective in its treatment of historical events. Gates also argues unconvincingly that the central river symbol is structurally and thematically inadequate ("Wordsworth's Mirror of Morality: Distortions of Church History," *Wordsworth Circle* [1981]: 129–32).

5. Wordsworth writes in the "Convention of Cintra" (1809):

"There is a spiritual community binding together the living and the dead: the good, the brave, and the wise of all ages. We would not be rejected from this community; and therefore do we hope" (W. J. B. Owen and Jane Worthington Smyser, eds., *The Prose Works of William Wordsworth* [New York: Oxford Univ. Press, 1974], 1:339).

6. Potts, 9.

7. Stephen Prickett, *Romanticism and Religion: The Tradition of Coleridge and Wordsworth in the Victorian Church* (New York: Cambridge Univ. Press, 1976), 254.

8. William Wordsworth to Reverend Francis Merewether, 29 Oct. 1833, *The Letters of William and Dorothy Wordsworth*, ed. Alan G. Hill, 7 vols. (New York: Oxford Univ. Press, 1979), 5:653. Hill points out that the request came probably from Archdeacon Bayley, not Benjamin Bailey as most critics have assumed (653n).

9. William Wordsworth to Samuel Wilkinson, 21 Sept. 1842, cited in Hill, 7:371.

10. Moorman, 2:482.

11. William Wordsworth to Crabb Robinson, 17 Jan. 1836, cited in Moorman, 2:482–83.

12. See Prickett, 255–56, for a discussion of the symbolic function of the Church in relation to the state.

13. *Methodist Quarterly Review* 21 (1839): 449–61, cited in Annabel Newton, *Wordsworth in Early American Criticism* (Chicago: Univ. of Chicago Press, 1928), 121–22.

14. William Wordsworth, *Ecclesiastical Sonnets*, in John O. Hayden, ed. *William Wordsworth: The Poems*, 2 vols. (New Haven, Conn.: Yale Univ. Press, 1981), III.47. Unless otherwise noted, further references to the poetry, relevant prefatory material, and accompanying notes of Wordsworth are from this edition and will appear parenthetically in the text when necessary.

15. Richard E. Brantley, *Wordsworth's "Natural Methodism"* (New Haven, Conn.: Yale Univ. Press, 1975), 138.

16. See Moorman 2:391–92 for a discussion of Wordsworth's love of churches.

17. Geoffrey Hartman, *Wordsworth's Poetry, 1784–1814* (New Haven, Conn.: Yale Univ. Press, 1964), 337.

18. Hoxie Neale Fairchild, *1730–1830: Romantic Faith*, vol. 3 of *Religious Trends in English Poetry* (New York: Columbia Univ. Press, 1949), 227–28.

Hartman discusses Wordsworth's "decline" and the *Ecclesiastical Sonnets*. He writes rather grudgingly that "before we add to [the many theories on Wordsworth's decline] it should be said that his later poetry is not uninteresting. . . . [I]t [has] a character of its own. . . . A falling-off is painfully obvious, however." He also quotes Crabb Robinson's 1827 comment: "This great poet survived to the fifth decade of the nineteenth century, but he appears to have died in the year 1814 as far as life consisted in an active sympathy with the temporal welfare of his fellow creatures" (*The Unremarkable Wordsworth* [Minneapolis: Univ. of Minnesota Press, 1987], 14–15).

In contrast to Robinson, A. D. Martin writes in 1836 that "the significance of *The Ecclesiastical Sonnets*" lies in the "recognition that Religion safeguards our humility best when it shows us that stored up in history, in liturgy, in the priestliness of saints, is the food we need for amplitude of soul. . . . [The *Ecclesiastical Sonnets*] have been disparaged by some as instancing the narrowing of Wordsworth's life when poetic inspiration failed him. In reality they are evidence of an actual broadening of his sympathies, his growth in personality, as compared to the days when he wrote much better poetry" (*The Religion of Wordsworth* [London: George Allen and Unwin, 1936], 86–87).

19. William Sharp, *Sonnets of the Nineteenth Century* (London: Walter Scott, 1886), lxxii. *American Biblical Repository*, 2d ser., (January 1839) 1:226–38, cited in Newton, 122.

20. Moorman, 2:400.

21. William Wordsworth to Richard Sharp, 16 April 1822, in Hill, 3:119.

1. The Series in Context

1. Kenneth R. Johnston argues "that *The Recluse* exists, not as an unrealized idea, but as a coherent though incomplete body of interrelated texts." He does not, however, view the *Ecclesiastical Sonnets* as having any significant relationship to *The Recluse* (*Wordsworth and The Recluse* [New Haven, Conn.: Yale Univ. Press, 1984], xi).

2. *The Recluse*, I.754–76; published as lines 1–23 of the *Prospectus* to *The Excursion* (Hayden 1:37–38).

3. The cooperation between the elements of nature and the Church is portrayed forcefully by John Constable in his *View of Salisbury Cathedral from the Bishop's Grounds* (1826), in which the trees nurturingly frame, indeed embrace, but do not oppress or visually overpower the cathedral. The friendship between Wordsworth and Constable began in 1806 and continued to the painter's

death in 1837. Although they admired each other's work, there is no record that Wordsworth commented on this particular painting.

4. Florence Marsh presents a thorough discussion of Wordsworth's use of water imagery in *Wordsworth's Imagery: A Study in Poetic Vision* (Hamden, Conn.: Archon, 1963), 86–103.

5. Wordsworth points out in his note on the *Duddon* that "the power of waters over the minds of poets has been acknowledged from the earliest ages;—through the 'Flumina amem sylvasque inglorius' of Virgil down to the sublime apostrophe to the great rivers of the earth, by Armstrong, and the simple ejaculation of Burns (chosen, if I recollect right, by Mr. Coleridge, as a motto for his embryo 'Brook')" (Ernest De Selincourt and Helen Darbishire, eds., *The Poetical Works of William Wordsworth*, 2d ed., 5 vols. [New York: Oxford Univ. Press, 1954], 3:504).

For biblical references that may have influenced Wordsworth's use of water and river imagery, see particularly Genesis 2:10 and Revelation 14:2 and 22:1.

6. William Wordsworth, *The Prelude, or Growth of a Poet's Mind* (Text of 1805), 1933, ed. Ernest De Selincourt (New York: Oxford Univ. Press, 1966), XIII.40–65. Further references to this edition of *The Prelude* will appear parenthetically in the text.

7. William Wordsworth, "Preface to Lyrical Ballads, with Pastoral and Other Poems (1802)," in Hayden, 1:886.

8. Harper, 565.

9. An interesting example of a culture that actually strives not to distinguish between past, present, and future is discussed in an anthropological study of the South Sea islanders by Dorothy Lee ("Codifications of Reality," *Psychosomatic Medicine* 12 [May 1950]: 157–71).

2. Part I: Reader Orientation—The Epigraph and Introductory Sonnets

1. To every natural form, rock, fruit or flower,
   Even the loose stones that cover the high-way,
   I gave a moral life, I saw them feel,
   Or link'd them to some feeling: the great mass
   Lay bedded in a quickening soul, and all
   That I beheld respired with inward meaning.
           (*Prelude* 1805.III.124–29)

2. Bishop White was ordained in 1787, and during his service, he consecrated twenty-six bishops in America.

3. Wordsworth's notes to the series include references to the following writers of historical works: Bede, G. Burnet, S. Daniel, G. W. Doane, G. Dyer, J. Foxe, T. Fuller, D. Hume, E. Stillingfleet, J. Strype, S. Turner, I. Walton, T. D. Whitaker, C. Wordsworth. The notes to Potts' critical edition of the series demonstrate, in most cases convincingly, that Wordsworth's sources were even more numerous.

3.   The Sonnet Set and Coherence Within the Series:
     Sonnets I.3 to I.5

1. Even the poet's notes to the sonnets direct the reader's attention to interconnections within the series. Wordsworth's note to line six of sonnet I.2 connects this sonnet with one in the middle of Part II: "The later part of this Sonnet refers to a favourite notion of Roman Catholic writers, that Joseph of Arimathea and his companions brought Christianity into Britain, and built a rude church at Glastonbury; alluded to hereafter, in a passage upon the dissolution of Monasteries [II.21]."

2. Although the Hayden edition of Wordsworth's works annotates "the Julian spear" as a reference to Emperor Julian (Flavius Claudius Julianus), who ruled from A.D. 361 to 363, "Julian" is clearly the poet's adjectival reference to Julius Caesar (c. 100–44 B.C.), whose conquest of Gaul brought the southern tribes of Britain under Roman influence. The first Roman conquest of the island occurred in A.D. 43 under Emperor Claudius (10 B.C.–A.D. 54).

Wordsworth knew history too well to attribute to Emperor Julian the opening of Britain to Christianity because, despite the undeniable mystery that surrounds the origin, the presence of Christianity in Britain is documented before Julian's reign (see Appendix C). Furthermore, if the poet meant "Julian's spear," that is probably what he would have written; if he meant "Julius' spear," the sibilance would have driven him to what appears in the sonnet, "the Julian spear."

3. The oldest known monastery in Britain is Celtic, existing now as ruins on the north Cornish coast, and dates from before A.D. 500 (David L. Edwards, *Christian England* [Grand Rapids, Mich.: Eerdmans, 1983], 1:28).

4. The next detailed scene that has painterly qualities, though neither to the extent, nor in the landscape tradition of sonnet I.5, appears in sonnet I.10, "Struggle of the Britons against the Barbarians." Two subsequent painterly sonnets, though of portraits, are

sonnet I.15, "Paulinus," and sonnet I.21, "Seclusion," which describes a "war-worn Chieftain" in monastic retirement.

5. Most importantly, in three biblical references, God, the Holy Ghost, and the Spirit are referred to as descending "as a dove" (as in Matthew 3:16, Luke 3:22, and John 1:32). To give some idea of the frequency of bird imagery in the Bible, there are thirty-two references to doves, seventy-four to birds, twenty to sparrows— but interestingly, only two to the cormorant (Leviticus 11:17 and Deuteronomy 14:17) and none to the sea-mew or seagull.

6. The poet points out in his note that the sea-mew "was, among the Druids, an emblem of those traditions connected with the deluge that made an important part of their mysteries." The druids believed that a flood had been sent to punish humankind and that the earth was repopulated by a righteous ruler who had been saved in a ship. As a white bird, the sea-mew may also be associated with purity and hope.

7. Light and dark are recurrent images in the King James Bible with 420 references to light, lighted, lighteth, lighting, lightning, lights, and 223 references to dark, darkened, darkness, darksome. Light is, of course, important in Genesis, where it is created, with six references. But the major frequencies occur, for both light and dark, in Job (33 light/26 dark), Isaiah (26 light/18 dark), John (25 light/11 dark), and Psalms (22 light/15 dark).

4. "For the Word . . . Yields Power": The Role of Language in Sonnets I.6 to I.14

1. Germanus had been sent to Britain in 430 to deal with the Pelagian heresy. He was eventually canonized. The story is told by Bede, an eighth-century Benedictine monk. Wordsworth was acquainted with Bede's fascinating account, provided in Appendix B.

2. The full quotation of this translated passage from Taliesin is as follows:

> I saw the oppression of the tumult; the wrath and tribulation;
> The blades gleaming on the bright helmets;
> The battle against the Lord of Fame in the dales of Hafren;
> Against Brocvail of Powys, who loved my muse.

(Sharon Turner, *History of the Anglo-Saxons*, 3d ed. [London, 1820], 1:322n, cited in Potts, 220)

3. Wordsworth writes in the "Convention of Cintra" (1809),

"There is a spiritual community binding together the living and the dead: the good, the brave, and the wise of all ages. We would not be rejected from this community; and therefore do we hope" (Owen, 1:339). In *The Prelude* Wordsworth writes,

> There is
> One great Society alone on earth,
> The noble Living and the noble Dead.
> (1805.X.968–70)

5.   The Sanctuary of Faith: Sonnets I.15 to I.25

   1.   Trees ("winter trees" in sonnet I.19; "decaying trunk" and "ancient elm" in sonnet I.21; and "sylvan arches cool," "beechen bowl," and "maple dish" in sonnet I.22); birds ("eagle's beak" in sonnet I.15; "Sparrow" and "wing" in sonnet I.16; and "hooting owl" and "crested fowl" in sonnet I.22); water ("fresh streams" in sonnet I.17; "brook," "mountain cove," and "translucent pool" in sonnet I.22; "wild coast" in sonnet I.23; "rains" in sonnet I.24; and "barbarous shores" in sonnet I.25); vegetation ("oblivious weeds" in sonnet I.17; "fruit" in sonnet I.19; "ivy," "fair growth," and "perennial bower" in sonnet I.21; "crisp, yellow leaves" in sonnet I.22; "grove or flowery mead" in sonnet I.23; and "palms" in sonnet I.24); related to vegetation ("living rock" in sonnet I.22 and "seeds of life" in sonnet I.25); weather ("wintry tempest" and "cold to cold" in sonnet I.16; "blaze / Of the noon-day" in sonnet I.18; and "sunshine" in sonnet I.24); and animals other than birds (an indirect reference to a horse in sonnet I.17; indirect references to serpents in sonnet I.21; and "bees" in sonnet I.24). The pervasiveness of nature imagery, rather than competing with the historical narrative, supports it and fleshes it out, making the past and the Church as accessible and organic as the natural world itself.
   2.   According to Bede:

> Another of the king's chief men signified his agreement with this prudent argument, and went on to say: "Your Majesty, when we compare the present life of man on earth with that time of which we have no knowledge, it seems to me like the swift flight of a single sparrow through the banqueting-hall where you are sitting at dinner on a winter's day with your thanes and counsellors. In the midst there is a comforting fire to warm the hall; outside, the storms of winter rain or snow are raging. This sparrow flies swiftly in through one door of the hall, and out through another. While he is inside, he is safe from the

winter storms; but after a few moments of comfort, he vanishes from sight into the wintry world from which he came. Even so, man appears on earth for a little while; but of what went before this life or of what follows, we know nothing. Therefore, if this new teaching has brought any more certain knowledge, it seems only right that we should follow it." (*A History of the English Church and People,* trans. Leo Sherley-Price, ed. R. E. Latham [New York: Dorset, 1985], 2.13)

Biblical passages pertaining to sparrows that may have inspired this image are Matthew 10:29–31, Luke 12:6–7, and Psalms 84:3.

3. In this group of sonnets several words or images continue to resonate from previous sonnets. For instance, the "bare words" of St. Augustine in sonnet I.14 make an interesting connection with "bare . . . trees," referring to clergy in sonnet I.19; and then a tree is used in sonnet I.21 as an analogy to the cloistered chieftain's mental life ("Round the decaying trunk of human pride"). The image modulates, merging language with nature and nature with humanity. Some of the echoes serve as reminders of the character of the time: "wild shores" in sonnet I.2; "unconscious shores" in sonnet I.14; "barbarous shores" in sonnet I.25; and reference to weapons in sonnets I.3, I.6, I.12, I.14, I.17, and I.21. Themes and images are repeated as if to remind the reader of the interrelationship of the work's parts. The forgotten language of Babylon in sonnet I.25 recalls the replacement of the Celtic language with Latin in sonnet I.12. The cloistered war-worn chieftain in sonnet I.21, who spends his time in "penitential cogitations," juxtaposes, in part, the Welsh bards in sonnet I.10 who relinquish their words for swords. The cloistered chieftain's life also serves as an option to others, given the violent state of affairs. The weeds in the sonnet on conversion, I.17, will echo in the sonnet on baptism, III.20.

A few examples in sonnet I.22 of echoes from other works are "beechen bowl" (*Prelude* 8.344); "maple dish" (*Excursion* V.687); "owl" (*Excursion* VI.327); and "thorp . . . vill" (*Excursion* VIII.100).

4. There are other examples of the influence of streams on Wordsworth's psychic life: In *The Prelude,* the Derwent's "ceaseless music . . . compos'd [his] thoughts . . . giving [him] . . . / A knowledge . . . of the calm / That Nature breathes among the hills and groves" (1805.I.279–85). In "Tintern Abbey," the bank of a stream becomes the point of memory and association:

> Nor, perchance—
> If I should be where I no more can hear
> Thy voice, nor catch from thy wild eyes these gleams

Of past existence—wilt thou then forget
That on the banks of this delightful stream
We stood together; and that I, so long
A worshipper of Nature, hither came
Unwearied in that service; rather say
With warmer love—oh, with far deeper zeal
Of holier love. Nor wilt thou then forget,
That after many wanderings, many years
Of absence, these steep woods and lofty cliffs,
And this green pastoral landscape, were to me
More dear, both for themselves and for thy sake!
                                                (146–59)

In addition, a reference to an echo in the mind appears early in
The Prelude: "the mind's / Internal echo of the imperfect sound"
(1805.I.64–65).
    5. Compare this consciousness of being to the blessed mood,
which is nurtured by memory in "Tintern Abbey" (41–49). Another
connection between the soul and perception is demonstrated in
Peter Bell, although here it is the soul of nature: "Let good men feel
the soul of nature, / And see things as they are" (764–65).
    The emphasis placed on the body and the senses in this sonnet
set may reflect the poet's interest in the fundamental theological
issue involving the relationship between the senses and the spirit,
especially in regard to the Eucharist. The following theological argument from Steinmetz's *Luther in Context* may highlight some of the
poet's possible concerns in writing this section of the series:

> The central message of the Bible is that God is found in dust, that the
> Second Person of the Trinity has taken humanity in Jesus of Nazareth.
> God always comes to men and women in creaturely elements that they
> can see, touch, and handle. That does not mean that his saving presence
> is self-evident to human reason or that his glory is visible. Just as the
> flesh of Jesus Christ is the *figura* or form under which the divine nature
> is hidden, so too are the bread and wine *figurae* or forms under which
> the body and blood are hidden. The reality of the divine presence is
> always hidden under the form of a contrary appearance. In that sense,
> the incarnation and the eucharist are exactly parallel. No objection can
> be alleged against the doctrine of the real presence which cannot be
> alleged equally well against the incarnation itself. To say "this signifies
> my body" is to obscure the reality of the incarnational principle. The
> bread and wine are not a sign of the body of Christ (*figura* in Oecolam-

padius' sense) but the form under and through which the body is offered
to the communicant. ([Bloomington: Indiana Univ. Press, 1986], 75)

6. William Wordsworth to Dorothy Wordsworth, 6 Sept. 1790,
cited in Christopher Wordsworth, *Memoirs of William Wordsworth*,
ed. Henry Reed (New York: AMS, 1966), 1:60.

7. References to breathing include "breathe a note" in sonnet
I.18; "breathe the common air" in sonnet I.19; and "breath" in sonnet
I.23. References to voice include "what a pensive Sage doth utter,
hear!" in sonnet I.15; "the inviting voice / Heard near fresh streams"
in sonnet I.17; "A benediction from his voice" in sonnet I.19; "dirges
sung" in sonnet I.20; and "Nor leaves her Speech one word to aid
the sigh / That would lament her" in sonnet I.25. References to the
body include "shoulders curved," "stature tall," "Black hair," "vivid
eye," "meagre cheek," and nose like an "eagle's beak" in sonnet I.15;
"Body" in sonnet I.16; "eyes," "necks," "voice or hand," and "heart"
in sonnet I.19; "Body," "tongue," "heart" in sonnet I.20; "his side,"
"hand," "locks" in sonnet I.21; "*My* feet" and "my sight" in sonnet
I.22; "creeping feet" and "passing breath" in sonnet I.23; and "step"
and "knee-worn floors" in sonnet I.25.

8. Wordsworth's note to sonnet I.23: "He expired dictating the
last words of a translation of St. John's Gospel." His source was T.
Fuller, *The Church History of Britain*, 3 vols. (London, 1837), cited
in Potts, 230.

9. The poet's ostensible longing for withdrawal from the world
recalls the Solitary in *The Excursion*.

10. Wordsworth discusses the role of Fancy in the "Preface to the
Poems (1815)" and in his note to "The Thorn" (Hayden, 2:907–23;
1:948–50).

11. One is reminded of "The World is Too Much With Us" (1802–
4):

> Great God! I'd rather be
> A Pagan suckled in a creed outworn;
> So might I, standing on this pleasant lea,
> Have glimpses that would make me less forlorn;
> Have sight of Proteus rising from the sea;
> Or hear old Triton blow his wreathed horn.

12. Contrast the negative effects of the supernatural in, for example, sonnets I.28, I.30, I.38, and I.39, having to do with abuses of
papal power.

13. Littledale, (*Wordsworth's Literary Criticism* [1905], 255),
cited in Potts, 228 n. 8–12.

6. Faith and Governance: A Fissure Between Nature and the
    Church in Sonnets I.26 to I.39

1. Potts provides interesting background on Wordsworth's use
of the oak tree:

> Wordsworth had often used or referred to this figure: *Convention of
> Cintra, Prose Works* I.227; *Westmoreland 2, Prose Works* 2.312. There
> was an oak at Michael's door (*Michael* 165). *The Oak of Guernica*, The
> Prior's Oak (*White Doe* 34), and the Lord's Oak (*Excursion* 7.622) were
> all associated in Wordsworth's mind with conceptions of dignity and
> power. To oak and sycamore he had compared the Wanderer and the
> Pastor (*Excursion* 5.455–61). The same 'forest oaks of Druid memory'
> (*Eccl. Son.* 3.39.7) had spread over the early Christian monks: The
> Field of Oaks, Dearmach [Durrow in Leinster], where Columba built
> a monastery (Bede, *Eccl. Hist.*, tr. by Sellar, p. 142), and Augustine's
> Oak (Fuller, *Ch. Hist.* 1.89). The Dedication (45–54) of *The White Doe*
> has the image of forest-tree, and tempest breaking over wide realms;
> and the picture of Emily under the leafless oak (*White Doe* 1629-38) is
> similar to the quiet ending of this sonnet. Cf. Virgil, *Georg.* 2.291–7.
> (235nn. 8–14)

2. George Macaulay Trevelyan, *A Shortened History of England*
(Baltimore, Md.: Penguin, 1976), 98.

3. According to Roland H. Bainton: "The leaders [of the cru-
sades] appeared more interested in carving kingdoms than in reaching the Holy City. Only the pressures from the papal party and the
common soldiers held the crusades together until they reached the
walls of Jerusalem. The city succumbed in 1099. The crusaders
waded to the fetlocks of their horses in the blood of the infidel, then
proceeded to the Church of the Holy Sepulcher, singing in jubilation
that Christ had conquered" (*Christendom: A Short History of Christianity and Its Impact on Western Civilization* [New York: Harper
and Row, 1966], 1:180–81).

7. Part II: The Synthetic Vision

1. Dorothy Wordsworth to Samuel Rogers, 3 Jan. 1823: "[In the
Sketches, my brother] likes best . . . the succession of [sonnets] on
the Reformation [probably sonnets II.29 to II.40], and those towards

the conclusion of the third part [probably sonnet III.34, the well-known 'Mutability,' and continuing with those on churches, cathedrals, and King's College Chapel]" (Hill, 4:180).

2. Significantly, "weeds" also appear in sonnet III.20, "Baptism."

8. Part III: Toward the Apocalypse—The New Eden in the Fallen World

1. The following sonnets from Parts I and II lend themselves to be read separately from the series: sonnet I.1, "Introduction"; sonnet I.12, "Monastery of old Bangor"; sonnet I.18, "Apology"; sonnet I.21, "Seclusion"; sonnet I.22, "Continued"; sonnet I.23, "Reproof"; sonnet I.30, "Canute"; sonnet I.38, "Scene in Venice"; sonnet II.9, "As faith thus sanctified the warrior's crest"; sonnet II.12, "The Vaudois"; sonnet II.16, "Wars of York and Lancaster"; sonnet II.17, "Wicliffe"; sonnet II.21, "Dissolution of the monasteries"; sonnet II.24, "Saints"; sonnet II.25, "The Virgin"; sonnet II.33, "Revival of Popery"; sonnet II.37, "English reformers in exile"; sonnet II.40, "The same," (a continuation of "Eminent reformers"); sonnet II.42, "Gunpowder Plot"; sonnet II.43, "Illustration: The Jung-Frau and the fall of the Rhine near Schaffhausen"; sonnet II.44, "Troubles of Charles the First"; and sonnet II.46, "Afflictions of England."

2. Wordsworth's note to sonnet III.18, cited in Potts, 291–92.

3. The Fenwick note states: "When I came to this part of the series, I had the dream described in this Sonnet. The figure was that of my daughter, and the whole passed exactly as here represented. The sonnet was composed on the middle road leading from Grasmere to Ambleside: it was begun as I left the last house of the vale, and finished, word for word as it now stands, before I came in view of Rydal."

4. Wordsworth's love of humanity and his country was intense. He literally sickened himself with worry over political issues, nearly panicking over the possible effects of the Reform Bill of 1832; his sister writes: "If it were not for the newspapers, we should know nothing of the turbulence of our great Towns and Cities. Yet my poor Brother is often heart-sick and almost desponding—and no wonder—for until this point at which we are arrived he has been a true prophet as to the course of events—dating from the 'Great Days of July' and the appearance of the Reform Bill. . . . If it were not for public affairs his spirits would be as cheerful as ever" (Dorothy Wordsworth to Crabb Robinson, 1 Dec. 1831, in Hill, 5:460).

5. Harper, 608.

6. Note a similar process in these lines from the Lucy poems. The first is from "Three Years She Grew in Sun and Shower":

Three years she grew in sun and shower,
Then Nature said, "A lovelier flower
On earth was never sown;
This Child I to myself will take"
. . . .
Thus Nature spake—The work was done—
How soon my Lucy's race was run!
She died, and left to me
This heath, this calm, and quiet scene;
The memory of what has been,
And never more will be.

(1–4, 37–42)

The second is from "A Slumber Did My Spirit Seal":

No motion has she now, no force;
She neither hears nor sees;
Rolled round in earth's diurnal course
With rocks, and stones, and trees.

(5–8)

7. The poet's praise in *The Prelude* for his mother's childrearing practices describes her trust in the ability, with God's help, to draw "Sweet honey out of spurned or dreaded weeds" (1850.V.278).
8. William Wordsworth in Christopher Wordsworth, 1:8.

Appendix C: Early Evidence of Christianity in Britain

1. Edwards, 1:22.
2. Edwards, 1:22.
3. Three according to Stephen Neill, *Anglicanism*, 4th ed. (New York: Oxford Univ. Press, 1982), 9.
4. Edwards, 1:21.
5. Edwards, 1:20.
6. Neill, 9.
7. Edwards, 1:20.
8. Edwards, 1:20.

Selected Bibliography

Primary Sources

De Selincourt, Ernest, ed. *The Prelude, or Growth of a Poet's Mind* (Text of 1805). 1933. Revised impression by Helen Darbishire. New York: Oxford Univ. Press, 1966.

De Selincourt, Ernest, and Helen Darbishire, eds. *The Poetical Works of William Wordsworth.* 2d ed. 5 vols. London: Oxford Univ. Press, 1952–59.

Hayden, John O., ed. *William Wordsworth: The Poems.* 2 vols. New Haven, Conn.: Yale Univ. Press, 1981.

Hill, Alan G., ed. *The Letters of William and Dorothy Wordsworth.* 7 vols. New York: Oxford Univ. Press, 1974–88.

Owen, W. J. B., and Jane Worthington Smyser, eds. *The Prose Works of William Wordsworth.* 3 vols. New York: Oxford Univ. Press, 1974.

Secondary Sources

Biography

Harper, George McLean. *William Wordsworth: His Life, Works and Influence.* New York: Scribner's, 1929.

Moorman, Mary. *William Wordsworth: A Biography.* 2 vols. New York: Oxford Univ. Press, 1957, 1965.

Reed, Mark L. *Wordsworth: The Chronology of the Early Years, 1770–1779.* Cambridge, Mass.: Harvard Univ. Press, 1967.

Wordsworth, Christopher. *Memoirs of William Wordsworth*. Edited
    by Henry Reed. 2 vols. New York: AMS, 1966.

Historical and Religious Texts

Bainton, Roland H. *Christendom: A Short History of Christianity
    and Its Impact on Western Civilization*. 2 vols. New York:
    Harper and Row, 1966.
Bede. *A History of the English Church and People*. Translated by
    Leo Sherley-Price. Edited by R. E. Latham. New York: Dorset,
    1985.
Butler, Joseph. *Analogy of Religion, Natural and Revealed, to the
    Constitution and Course of Nature*. Edited by J. T. Champlin.
    Boston: Bazin and Ellsworth, 1860.
Edwards, David L. *Christian England*. 3 vols. Grand Rapids, Mich.:
    Eerdmans, 1983, 1984.
Eusebius. *The History of the Church from Christ to Constantine*.
    Translated by G. A. Williamson. New York: Dorset, 1965.
Neill, Stephen. *Anglicanism*. 4th ed. New York: Oxford Univ. Press,
    1982.
Steinmetz, David C. *Luther in Context*. Bloomington: Indiana Univ.
    Press, 1986.
Trevelyan, George Macaulay. *A Shortened History of England*. Bal-
    timore, Md.: Penguin, 1976.

Literary Criticism

Abrams, M. H., ed. *Wordsworth: A Collection of Critical Essays*.
    Englewood Cliffs, N.J.: Prentice-Hall, 1972.
Batho, Edith. *The Later Wordsworth*. Cambridge: Cambridge Univ.
    Press, 1933.
Bauer, Neil Stephen, ed. *William Wordsworth: A Reference Guide
    to British Criticism, 1793–1899*. Boston: Hall, 1978.
Beatty, Arthur. *William Wordsworth: His Doctrine and Art in Their
    Historical Relations*. Madison: Univ. of Wisconsin Press, 1960.
Beatty, Frederika. *William Wordsworth of Rydal Mount*. London:
    Dent, 1939.
Bloom, Harold, ed. *Modern Critical Views: William Wordsworth*.
    New York: Chelsea, 1985.
Brantley, Richard E. *Wordsworth's "Natural Methodism."* New Ha-
    ven, Conn.: Yale Univ. Press, 1975.
Campbell, O. J. "Wordsworth's Conception of the Esthetic Experi-

ence." In *Wordsworth and Coleridge*, edited by E. L. Griggs, 26–46. Princeton, N.J.: Princeton Univ. Press, 1939.

Danby, John Francis. *The Simple Wordsworth*. New York: Barnes and Noble, 1961.

Davis, Jack, ed. *Discussions of William Wordsworth*. Boston: Heath, 1964.

Fairchild, Hoxie Neale. *Religious Trends in English Poetry*. Vol. 3, *1780–1830: Romantic Faith*. New York: Columbia Univ. Press, 1949.

Ferry, David. *The Limits of Mortality: An Essay on Wordsworth's Major Poems*. Middletown, Conn.: Wesleyan Univ. Press, 1959.

Hartman, Geoffrey. *The Unremarkable Wordsworth*. Minneapolis, Minn.: Univ. of Minnesota Press, 1987.

———. *Wordsworth's Poetry, 1784–1814*. New Haven, Conn.: Yale Univ. Press, 1964.

Johnson, Lee M. *Wordsworth and the Sonnet*. Copenhagen: Rosenkilde and Bagger, 1973.

Johnston, Kenneth R. *Wordsworth and the Recluse*. New Haven, Conn.: Yale Univ. Press, 1984.

Lindenberger, Herbert. *On Wordsworth's Prelude*. Princeton, N.J.: Princeton Univ. Press, 1963.

Logan, James V. *Wordsworthian Criticism: A Guide and Bibliography*. New York: Gordian, 1974.

Marsh, Florence. *Wordsworth's Imagery: A Study in Poetic Vision*. Hamden, Conn.: Archon, 1963.

Martin, A. D. *The Religion of Wordsworth*. London: Allen and Unwin, 1936.

Newton, Annabel. *Wordsworth in Early American Criticism*. Chicago: Univ. of Chicago Press, 1928.

Perkins, David. *The Quest for Resonance: The Symbolism of Wordsworth, Shelly, and Keats*. Cambridge: Harvard Univ. Press, 1959.

Pinion, F. B. *A Wordsworth Companion*. New York: Macmillan, 1984.

Potts, Abbie Findlay, ed. Introduction to *The Ecclesiastical Sonnets of William Wordsworth: A Critical Edition*. New Haven, Conn.: Yale Univ. Press, 1922.

Prickett, Stephen. *Romanticism and Religion: The Tradition of Coleridge and Wordsworth in the Victorian Church*. New York: Cambridge Univ. Press, 1976.

Purkis, John. *A Preface to Wordsworth*. London: Longman, 1970.

Sharp, William. *Sonnets of the Nineteenth Century*. London: Walter
    Scott, 1886.
Smith, Elsie. *An Estimate of William Wordsworth by His Contempo-
    raries, 1793–1822*. New York: Haskell, 1966.
Smith, J. C. *A Study of Wordsworth*. Edinburgh: Oliver and Boyd,
    1944.
Wesling, Donald. *Wordsworth and the Adequacy of Landscape*.
    London: Routledge and Kegan Paul, 1970.
Woodring, Carl. *Wordsworth*. Boston: Houghton Mifflin, 1965.
Wordsworth, Jonathan. *The Music of Humanity*. New York: Harper
    and Row, 1969.
Wordsworth, Jonathan, ed. *Bicentenary Wordsworth Studies in
    Memory of John Alban Finch*. Ithaca, N.Y.: Cornell Univ. Press,
    1970.

Index

Animals: in Bede, 52; bird imagery in Bible, 121n.5; birds, 38–39, 84; bird song, 41, 45–46, 62; colts, 93; cuckoo, 98–99; deer, 93; Dove, 93; in Isaiah, 107; as metaphor, 53–54; sanctuary for, 80; sea-mew, 121n.6; snake, 105; sparrow, 52, 63, 111, 122n.1, 122–23n.2

Apocalypse, 18, 26, 88–107; apocalyptic vision, 54–55, 105–6; relation between time and nature, 103

Atonement: Wordsworth's view of, xiii

Autobiographical sonnets, 22, 99. *See also* Beaumont, Sir George

Baptism, 18, 20, 26, 29–30, 52, 56–57, 63, 88, 90, 99, 112; call to, 60; of reader, 59; in sonnet III.20, 16, 98

Beaumont, Sir George: and Coleorton, origin of series, 3, 19, 22, 92

Bede, 16, 51, 57, 58, 62, 67, 121n.1, 122–23n.2; active life, 60; Hallelujah Victory, 112–13; sparrow passage, 52

Bible: bird imagery in, 121n.5; Genesis, 50, 105, 119n.5; Isaiah, 83, 106–7, 121n.7; John, 30, 50, 57, 60, 89, 125n.8; Job, 121n.7; Lamentations of Jeremiah, 49; landscape, 85; Luke, 16, 49; Mark, 49; Matthew, 47; Paul, 27; Peter, 27, 28; Psalms, 85, 121n.7; Revelation, 54, 105, 106, 119n.5; sparrows, 122–23.n2; Timothy, 59

Body: of Christ, 56–57; parts of, 125n.7; and soul, 56

Canonization, 75

Charity, 81, 83, 87

Childhood: loss of, 101

Children. *See* Death

Christian identity, xii, xvi, 14, 19, 21, 23–24, 26, 58, 87

Christianity: in Britain, early evidence of, 114

Christian mission: lost sight of, 66. *See also Ecclesiastical Sonnets*

Church: Anglican/Episcopal, 90; architectural presence, 1, 52;

given attributes of nature, 80,
83–84; calendar, 105; criticism
and praise of, 25, 66, 79–83;
fallibility of, 25; foundation of
nation, xiii, xiv; historical
research, 60; Idea of, 52;
institutional and private forms
of, 1; and landscape, 91, 92–96;
personalized history of, 54;
political concerns, 89; reforms,
79; rituals, 97; Rushbearing
ceremony, 90, 97; synthesizing
force, 3; unifying element, 63
Church, as a building: analogy to
Wordsworth's works, 15;
architectural element, 52;
building, 92, 96; erection of, 57;
and graveyards, 20; integrated
into landscape, 4, 15, 91, 94;
new, 88, 92; in sonnet III.38,
98; old and new, 91; old abbeys,
105; oldest known monastery,
120n.3; role in community, 90;
site for, 89; in sonnets III.39-41,
89; spires, 103; tower, 104;
Wordsworth's love of, 117n.16
Church and state: relationship, 65,
67; religion and nationalism, 76;
symbolic function, 117n.12;
undulation of power, 79
Clergy, 51; pastor, among flock,
95; responsibility of, 90; role in
community, 89; Saxon 53
Constable, John, 118n.3
Covenant, 20, 39
Critics: Batho, Edith, xv; Brantley,
Richard E., xiv, xv; Campbell,
O. J., xv; Fairchild, Hoxie Neal,
xv; Harper, George:
objectification of works, 10; on
death of Dora, 100; Hartman,
Geoffrey: on *Duddon*, xv; on
Ecclesiastical Sonnets, 117–
18n.18; Johnson, Lee M., xv;
Martin, A.D., xv; Moorman,
Mary, xiii, xv, xvi; Newton,

Annabel, xiv, xv; Potts, Abbie
Findlay, xii, xv; Sharp, William,
xvi; Wordsworth on
Ecclesiastical Sonnets, xvi
Crucifixion, 20, 32, 34
Crusades, 65, 76–77, 126n.3

Dead, burial of, 51
Death, 56; of child, 100–101; of
God, xv, 54; of Wordsworth's
children, 100–101; of
Wordsworth's mother and
father, 101
Doppelgänger, 58
Dream, 100; Wordsworth's, 127n.3
Druids, 35
Duddon: "After-thought," 89;
dedicated to Christopher
Wordsworth, 11; Hartman, xv;
river imagery, 49; theme, 11;
traces course of river, 4, 8–9;
water imagery, 119n.5
Duty, 24

Ecclesiastical Sketches: date of
publication, xi
Ecclesiastical Sonnets: accessibility
of Part III, xvi, 88, 90; and
canon, 3; Christian mission, 17,
66; coherence, 31–40, 60,
120n.1, 123n.3; in context of
other work, 17; drive toward
affirmation and synthesis, 3; epic
scope, 1; epigraph, 14–17;
motivations for writing, xiii;
number of sonnets, xi, 31;
originality, xi, 115–16n.1; origin
of, 3, 92; ostensible purpose, 16,
22, 116n.4; personal journey, 61;
praise of, 118n.18; prefatory
letter, xiii; prose attachments,
16; purpose of, xii, xiii–xiv, 14,
18, 21–24, 92; reconciliation, xv;
research for, 116n.3; sonnets to
be read separately from series,
127n.1; stand between humanity

39, 58, 81, 123–24n.4, 125n.5; "The World is Too Much with Us," 125n.11; "Yes, It Was the Mountain Echo," 98–99. *See also Duddon; The Prelude*

Worldview, 33, 52; Edenistic, 96, 105–6; interpenetration of spiritual and material worlds, 9; moral progress, xiv, xv, 11. *See also* Synthetic vision

Anne L. Rylestone is at the University of Massachusetts at Amherst, where she is the Assistant to the Dean of the Faculty of Humanities and Fine Arts and where she teaches in the Department of English and the Department of Comparative Literature. She is from Long Island, New York, where she started her teaching career, graduating with a bachelor's and a master's degree from the State University of New York at Stony Brook. Her doctorate is from the University of Massachusetts at Amherst.